Horace Eaton Walker

Acrisius, King of Argos

Horace Eaton Walker

Acrisius, King of Argos

ISBN/EAN: 9783337380106

Printed in Europe, USA, Canada, Australia, Japan

Cover: Foto ©ninafisch / pixelio.de

More available books at **www.hansebooks.com**

ACRISIUS, KING OF ARGOS,

AND OTHER POEMS

BY

HORACE EATON WALKER.

CONTENTS.

———

Acrisius, King of Argos.

DRAMATIS PERSONÆ.

ACRISIUS, *King of Argolis.*
DANÆ, *daughter of King Acrisius.*
APOLLO, *god of archery, prophesy and music.*
ZEUS, *king of gods, and husband of Danæ.*
DELIA, *wife of Acrisius.*
POLYDECTES, *King of Seriphus.*
DICTYS, *brother of Polydectes.*
PERSEUS. *only child of Danæ.*
ANDROMEDA, *celebrated for her beauty.*
HIPPODAMIA. *daughter of King of Pisa.*
BETTA, *Danæ's nurse.*
FELLDAFF, *a Grecian brazier.*
HARDSPUR, *a villain.*
BRASKER, *Hardspur's friend in crime.*
Attendants, heralds, soldiers, officers, etc.

ACT I.

SCENE 1.

In the Palace of King Acrisius. Evening. Enter the King of Argos and his wife.

King. To be the King of Argos is an honor:
But how much more the honor unto her,
As wife, who giveth unto him a son
To wear his father's crown, and be a king
From birth!
Queen. Aye! lord and master, 'tis e'en so:
And Queen of Argos yet will sit beneath
The pale white moon, and study how she may
Give to her proud old king a son, to be
A Nestor of the world!
King. 'Tis said, my queen!
And never old Saronic gulf of Argos
Saw proudlier woman than my queenly Delia,
In new ambition to become a mother.
Argolic gulf in watery song shall sing thee,
The fertile plain of Argolis shall join it,
The grand, the staid Malevo group of mountains,
The Artemision range, in courtly ditty,
Arcadian boundaries, circling in their wonder,
And kingdom in an everlasting homage.
Queen. Then will I make essay to do thy hest;
But yet has fairest Danæ blessed thy throne,
And with a queenly beauty rare indeed,
Rivalling the stars and rainbow and white moon,
Such is the splendor of her beauty.
King. Yes!
And grandeur's in the word. Indeed, I join

My queenliest wife in all her wisdom's verdict.
For, Delia, Danaë's truly Greek of Greeks,
And 's peer of any goddess.
  Queen.   Yet wilt ask
A rival from the womb that gave her birth!
  King. All men have whims, and e'en no less a king;
For though the stars do fall, I yet would have
A noble son, yea! grand as any. You
Alone of women fair can bear him yet;
And should he match by half our Danaë rare,
Then shall the world possess a god indeed.
For, look you, man may read of earthly Nestors,
The brave Achilles and the great Leanders,
Heroes and men in every human sense.
Would not the Queen of Argos bow to heaven
Had she gin birth to such a piece of manhood?
  Queen. Helen of Troy was such a masterpiece.
My Danaë 's peer of any heroine!
  King. Well said, my wondrous wife. But mine 's ambition
Only the great kings can wot of; for kings
Are more than queens.
  Queen.   Then I, once Delia fair,
The queen and wife of Argos's greatest monarch,
Wilt study well new motherhood, and be
The willing harbinger within the year
Of King of Argos's kingly son!
  King.   'Tis now
Thou art my wife indeed. and do I bless thee
With kingly kisses, and a man's regard
Who feels his wife will conquer on a field
Where doughty captains are outgeneraled.
For look ye back in history; men have risen
On field of battle, mighty soldiers. Queens
Have risen also in ye olden empires.
But man 's a mightier, for a woman 's less
In fair comparison, at best, with man.
  Queen. It may be so; but Danaë is my idol.
  King. And well. But, sit beside me while I paint
The nuptials of our wedding morn, when first
I led thee captive maid through Cupid's wiles
To Hymen's marriage altar. Thou didst shine
With supernatural lustre; and our union
Bespoke a unison of two young hearts
That throbbed in one harmonious tune. And, therefore,
No wonder grew that Danaë was so fair,
So meet, and all endowed with native beauty,
E'en rivalling renowned Andromeda.
  Queen. 'Twas only love that swayed us then, Acrisius.
The potencies of state and governmental
Law had but smallest part. King Eros reigned.
  King. And so today. But kings grow old, and Danaë
Is only offspring of our stately house;
And this should never hap. A courtly son,
With splendid 'contrements of face and form;
And manly prestige, with a lineal line

Of blood that has coursed thro' kings' veins for years
Now unremembered, sith so long ago
Their first beginning, shouldst e'en soon be added
To King Acrisius's house. O, dost agree,
My queen and long enduring wife? Speak out.
 Queen. Already has she spoken. Her will 's thine.
But, King Acrisius, nay full years of harvest
Are past and 'yond recall, unless the gods
Are part propitiated in our favor.
 King. Confusion! So they are. I'll hie me hence
Tomorrow, and consult the oracle
Of god Apollo.
 Queen.   Do so soon. Enlist
His favor; and may all consenting gods
Propitious bow to his decree.
 King.   Then, wife,
I bid thee now a kingly faretheewell;
I'd hence to count the moments 'neath the stars
As one by one they build the happy hour
That see'st me father of a son. Good by,
And faretheewell, my own, my loveliest queen;
And may the gods of earth and starry heaven
Still bless thy fleeting hours with kingly plenty.
 Queen. By all the classic waves of Inachus,
The babbling waters of old Kephalari,
Thy Delia 'll do her wifely duties; and
Heaven sparing and extending her divinity,
Her age shall bless the throne of King Acrisius
With such a son that men shall say: The Queen
Of Argos, in her fall of life, has given
Her king such son the world hath not a peer.
 King. Bravo! Adelia. This is eloquence:
And do I swear by old Arcadian mountains,
Proud Phlius and Cleonæ and Corinthia,
And hoary Peloponnesus, thou art
My wife, a thing not often said by kings;
And all the kingdoms of old Argolis,
Mycenæ and Hermione and Tiryns,
Shalt hear our double glory, rarest queen,
And ministering angel to my earthly greatness.
 Queen. May Jove's great stars smile on our high ambition.
 King. And all good deities of earth and sky.   [*Ex. Queen.*
A star of night she saileth from my ken,
A woman that's a boon to kings or men.
Now will I forth in twilight shades and talk
Of her and self and joy that's soon to be.
The birds are hushed. All nature's in repose,
And, save the teasing brooks aneath the moon
That rides on yonder hill, no sound is heard.
The snakes are noiseless in the grass. How calm,
How placid is the hour of night! Alone
With God I stand amid the freighted twilight,
The King of Argos, greatest of his line.
I came upon the throne direct in blood,
And now am old in honored reign. But, Argos,

Old Argolis, to make me ripe with earth
Renown, and more than kingly glory, I
Shalt raise a son as noble as the stars,
As high, to fill the place I 've filled so well.
Lying alone, as 't were, old Argos sleeps
Atween the bays of Nauplia and Ægina,
The greatest kingdom of old Greece, the greatest
King reigning as Acrisius. Forsooth,
To be the king of this peninsula,
Is noble, but to be the father of
A son is nobler! So, O Plain of Argos!
And Peloponnesus e'en guarding now,
As years, the riven coast and Lernean Marsh,
And Nome of old Morea, wilt bless me, king,
With son of woman! Then will I a ruler
Of Argolis, go forth and tame the Hydra,
And kill the Nemean lion; and O sea!
Thou everlasting memory of the past,
Yet hear my compact. And, fair Juno, list,
Cleonæ, Philus, Sicyon and old Trœzen,
And all the Doric states, for I am young
Again when thoughts like these do cross my brain,
That I 'm to be the father of a son! [*Ex. King.*

SCENE II.

Queen in Danæ's room.

Danæ. Good mother, pray wilt tell me why art come?
Queen. A plot is working in the good king's brain.
Danæ. Ah! good my mother, and the plot 's of evil?
Queen. Nay, daughter Danæ, in your room I say:
The goodly king 's ambitious in his years.
Danæ. But 't is not like him since I grew a child.
Queen. And never since I mind me of the hour
That made him king, and king of Argolis.
Then his ambition sought the skies; and not
Until the glittering crown descended on
His head, did proud Acrisius look amen!
But now, my Danæ, hast a new ambition
Befuddled his old brain.
Danæ. -   My mother dear,
And gray in earthly goodness, let thy Danæ,
Though yet a child, find solace for thy breast;
For care and worry make new shadows on
Thy face. Come, sit beside me, for I mind
The days when you were beauty's second self,
Tall and commanding, with a grandeur I
Did rank among the queens of Greece. Dost smile?
But never woman came to kingly home,
And sceptered throne, more born to them than thee;
And had my worthy father lost his mind,
And babbled in his talk, you 'd ta'en the reins
Of empire, and so patterned after him
In all his former glory, other kingdoms,
Near, far, had heard your queenly sovereignty,
And men had said: Behold a woman who

Is peer of any man, and reigns with splendor
In husband's stead o'er all the towns of Argos!
 Queen. From any other child than thee such news
Had fallen dead. But thou, sweet child, art true
As gold to me; and mayst thou ever be
As priceless with the lustre of true girlhood.
 Danæ. Flattery is not a part of Danæ's being.
 Queen. No, no; and 't were a pity one so fair,
And full of nature's goodliest store, of love,
And beauty, comeliness and stateliness,
With majesty of personality,
That make her fit to be the Queen of Argos,
Should be deposed by so ungracious sire.
 Danæ. A queen!
 Queen.   Indeed, a queen!
 Danæ.   But father lives.
The king still lives.
 Queen.   But kings are not immortal.
Like mortals they must die. Their crowns are not
A guarantee of life. Dread death is more
Than kings and kingdoms. He, Acrisius,
Is in his dotage.
 Danæ.   Mother, why these riddles?
Art thou the Sphinx?
 Queen.   No, Danæ, life to me
Was never more of life than now; for he,
The king, thy sire, would throw thee on the world.
Danæ. What! turn me forth, the offspring of his house,
And only blood-line to the throne at his
Demise?
 Queen. But hear me. I am wildered too,
As he is wildered. Forty years have been
Our wedded harvest, and till now he was
Content.
 Danæ. Has father as the King of Argos
Lost sway?
 Queen. Nay, nay, his reign is bright as steel.
 Danæ. And he is well?
 Queen.   He drinks his wine with gusto,
And leads the butler at a steak.
 Danæ.   What then?
Affairs unhinged? His government awry?
 Queen. All things move on as smooth as brooks of oil.
Courtier and noble, servant, knight and lord,
Move in and out like trained automatons,
So perfect is the order of his reign.
 Danæ. And he is yet unhappy?
 Queen.   Yea. One hour
Ago, the hundred thousand souls in Argos
Were never happier.
 Danæ.   He is wroth with thee?
 Queen. I prithee no. A very honeymoon
He'd make me. But, thy ear, my Danæ child,
The King of Argos once again would be
A father.

Dana.   Fie! a father? Passing folly.
Tomorrow 'll find him staid, sedate and grand,
A king of kings, with wisdom 'yond his age,
The age in which he lives, with cautious eye
To note the rise and fall of waves of state,
And guide with equal hand the helm of Argos.

Queen.   Well said, my own queen child; but till he know
If time do grant his folly-wish, he sleeps
Not on white beds of down, but on a rack
With angry glittering spikes to pierce his flesh.

Dana.   And argument has no avail? A word
Of wisdom naught of power? E'en blindly he
Will do his will, and all the gods, his thoughts,
Yet fail to pacify? I'm young in years,
And have presumption in my present act;
But, mother mine, I do advise thee not
To act in coldness, change a shade, a shred,
From present self. If any change, do act
As sunshine to his thought, and with him pray
For promised minute that shall see me sister
Unto a baby brother.

Queen.   Danae mine,
Thou 'rt wise beyond thy years, and ere I sleep,
I 'll so adjust my thoughts that my old face
Will not betray my bitter pain; for hear:
It 's not for self, for Argos or its people,
But thee, thee, thee!

Dana.   Then, mother, shed no tears,
For Danae has no thought save thee. Tomorrow,
Tonight, I 'd lay my head alow for thee;
Tonight, I 'd stand up 'gainst the god of death
For thee. Tonight, I 'd rise up face to face
And say: Thou art my father; but, king, she 's
My mother! Back! or thou shalt kill me first!
But, good my mother, leave me now for dreams
Of future happiness.

Queen.   E'en so I will,
And in those dreams still dream my dreams of thee.

Dana.   And sleep as newborn babe on mother's breast,
Thoughtless in idle dreams, if such they have.

Queen.   My blessing on thee, and my prayer is this:
That Danae maid may never have a brother.   [*Ex. Queen.*

Dana.   And never proudlier woman looked to God
For suave commiseration of her woe.
I 'll hie myself to god Apollo. He
Shalt hear my eloquence in stout behalf
Of that pure mother who did suckle me.
Father, the king, is in lamented state.
So long his reign, and unadulterated
With dross or weakness, and no near approach,
I can but little reck his present changes.
I have no mind to understand. So, dreams,
And prayers, and all good elfs, preside tonight,
That I on morrow morn may sway the god
Of wisdom, 'gainst the king, my father. It

In part consoles me that I have no motive
Other than truest love for her who bore me.   [*Ex. Danæ.*

SCENE III.

At the shrine of Apollo on Mount Delphi.

Apollo. These times be full of worldly wisdom, and
From Delos where I grew a babe, a lad,
The son of Jupiter and dark Latona,
I rose as fair Diana's brother to
Old Delphi, celebrated for its fame,
And world-renownèd oracle, until
I 'm now the sought-out Sun-god of the earth.
My word is law. No more I need to slay
The Python monsters. Fame is mine by laws
Inviolate as sun and moon. Once gained,
My petty word and whispered syllable,
Find ready credence. Did I say: O Man!
Thy span is brief. But two short decades thou
Wilt be o'erswept by mightier gods than I,
And all this earth of rock, and sea, and land.
The mammoth, mastodon and polar bear,
And every breathing thing, with man the highest,
Wilt be o'erwhelmed and crumbled into naught,
With never a vestige left behind to tell
The perished story. Yet I reign at Delphi.
And suns roll into space; the stars do come
And white o'ersprinkle all the lurid sky.
The rains do fall, and clouds in grand procession
Like some majestic host, march through the sky,
And disappear in wonder and great glory.
The seasons come and go in ordered train,
And now is Spring with beauty borrowed from
The firmament to deck this lesser world,
And paint a thousand fulgencies for day,
The rainbow's rival in its beautiful
And rarest intermixture of new colors.
Then cometh summer drowsed in odorous sweetness,
Zephyr and gale o'erladen with a balm
From heaven's Paradise, till human minds
Do wonder if the skies of God do hold
A lovelier. Then old Autumn, ripe in fruit
And wise maturity, still groweth sere
In fourfold plenteousness till old barns
And goodly garners, creak and strain and labor
With golden harvests. Then the winds come on
From frozen corners, hills and unsunned nooks,
And in the frozen morn a winding-sheet
Of snow now glitters in the frosty air,
And nature sleeps. To us the world seems dead,
But no! The spring returns, the summer comes,
And autumn; and for thousand years 't will be,
Hath been. Who comes? 'Tis beauty's self, and she
Has summer on her face, but stormy clouds
O'ershadow!
    Enter Danæ.

Danæ. O great Sun-god of old Delphi,
Wilt aught deny me audience here? I 've climbed
This hoary mount with ribbèd rock and stone,
And grandeur piercing heaven, and a glory
Renowned o'er all the world, to ask of thee
Some intercession in behalf of Delia,
My pure queen mother, and a woman rare.
 Apollo. Speak, fairest imitation of the angels,
Apollo's ear is ope to beauty's haps.
 Danæ. Some twenty years agone I came a babe,
As millions long before me, only I
Am Danæ, King Acrisius's only daughter.
 Apollo. Nay! 't is not heaven to be a king's own daughter.
And yet, proceed. And all the glitter here
Of gold and silver, amethyst and diamonds,
And twisted beauties from the Orient,
And velvets, plush, and all the decoration
Of human skill and earth despoiled of, daunt
Thee not.
 Danæ. Apollo, hear me as thy child,
As blood of blood, as richest ichor flowed
Within my veins. For I would near thy heart,
And make my case thy own.
 Apollo.   Proceed. Thy voice
Hath maiden melody!
 Danæ.   Till yesternight.
The king, my father, now of Argolis,
Happy did rest that I, his only child,
Still lived to take the Argos throne at his
Demise, and reign with new acquirèd wisdom.
 Apollo. Thou 'rt born a queen. Thy lineaments do show it,
And comely prestige of thy native presence.
 Danæ. But ere the farway stars came out and birds
And birds did hush their tantalizing melodies,
He swelled with kingly wisdom to become
Once more a father!
 Apollo.   'T is his second childhood.
He 'll be within his grave within the year,
If signs do keep their wonted course. But, Danæ,
Still sleep as sleep the innocent of earth.
 Danæ. And he would have the babe a boy, O Phœbus!
 Apollo. But, child, thy mother 's long since past such things.
Her duties all are now performed, save living
And honoring her and hers with such a presence
As Grecian woman ne'er has shown since Greece
First led the world with beauty and high honor.
 Danæ. But, God of Delphi, my strange sire would come
To thee for such a kind of intervention
Of all thy powers that this great woman once
Again shalt give birth to a child, a boy!
 Apollo. Go rest in peace. I'll meet thy father's wills
With such a kind of wisdom as may teach
Him kinglier sense. Go, go thou forth and wait;
For he who waits in patience wins at last.
 Danæ. I thank thee in behalf of her who bore me,

And her who bears the name of Danae. And
I leave thee in thy greatest glory, king
Of heaven and earth; and as to starry god,
Myself I bow from thee, O great Apollo!   [*Ex. Danae.*
    Apollo. They whisper of the beauty of the skies,
The heavens, and angels that do wing their way
Through fragrant space, their heads encrowned by stars
That shine in heaven. But Danae is a being
To tease their selfishness, if angels have
Such earthy trait. For she is beauty's self,
So will I call my art, and teach Acrisius
That nature's laws are still inviolate.
Forsooth, a son! Such thoughts are addle. I
Will wait the coming of this would-be father.
    Enter the King of Argolis.
    King. I bow till rainbow's yellow arch is emblem
Of old Acrisius's trite obsequiency,
For such his veneration of a god.
    Apollo. And I will give thee bow for bow; sith kings
Do seldom meet, such is their native rivalry.
    King. I'm but a dwarf beside an one so high
As thee; for Argos is but tract of God's
Wide earth, while thou'rt a king of earth and sky,
And have a superhuman power not mine,
Or any king's of any town of Greece!
    Apollo. I know my station. Some do not! Old men
Grow foolish in their years, and cry like children
For heaven's white stars. That every man could die,
And kings of kingdoms in especial, ere
Their second childhood make them babbling fools.
    King. What meanest thou? Mine second childhood? Mine
Lost wisdom? The great King of Argolis?
Nay, nay, my lord and king.
    Apollo.   Thy words shall answer,
Sith give a fool the hemp, he'll hang himself.
Give kings their tongues and old court clowns will smile.
    King. With quirks, vagaries, riddles thou dost tease me.
    Apollo. Thou hast thy tongue. Are all thy words of wisdom?
    King. Till now did never man impeach my greatness.
    Apollo. Till now thou wast great. Many a king's in dotage
Wide years before he dreams it. Man does lose
His head more oft than woman. My prediction
Shall find a verification ere the sun
Do mount the background hills of Argolis.
    King. In wise obeisance to an inner thought
I've come to thee. Wilt audience give that I
May short express that thought?
    Apollo.   I'm here to serve
Both sense and reason.
    King.   Both I'll try to show.
For never grandlier thoughts have passed the heads
Of kings.
    Apollo. But, harken. Is't not writ that kings
Are wiser than their subjects? Dost deny it?
    King. Nay, nay, for kings do make the world. The rabble,

The throng would be disunion and disorder,
With ruling kings dethroned. How oft the wisdom
Is put to test of wisest kings to keep
The empire right?
   Apollo.   And is the King of Argos
A king of this great line?
   King.   His have beens are
As proverbs told from mouth to mouth, their wisdom
Is such. But, pardon, god of Delphi. kings
Should meet on equal terms.
   Apollo.   The great kings do.
   King. I 'm but a king of Argos, a mere span
Of land to thee unknown. While thou art god
Of heaven and earth. So, bow I now to thee
As one, the only one with power to aid me
In all my newest plans.
   Apollo.   Then out! What wilt thou?
   King. I 've one fair daughter lovely as the rose.
She 's queen of beauty, with the limbs for noblest
Sculpture; and Danaë's presence is to me
A benison of loveliness, a something
That wooes, and lures, and wins. She is a queen!
   Apollo. A queen? This Danaë queen? For queens are few
And far not on a throne. But, list! she 'll soon
Be queen!
   King.   Apollo!
   Apollo.   For the marks of age
Already show their furrowed lines.
   King.   O god
Of Delos, time rests lightly on my face.
I 'm almost a young lad again. To dance,
To sing, to play, to be a father, yea!
To be a father!
   Apollo.   All thy talk is chatter.
You do but babble like a poor old man.
Recall the proverbs of thine earliest days.
For repetition 's better than a silly
Word.
   King. Speech is tangled in my buoyancy
Of new delight that I am soon to be
A father! For didst thou not promise it?
   Apollo. A father? Promise? Thou art past the hour!
   King. O god of Pytho! hold such declaration,
It is the one ambition of my life,
The hope of my decline. My life's one thought.
   Apollo. But Delia, thy true wife, is barren as
Pasture fields. Danaë 'll fill thy place as perfect
As living woman, more than thy own son;
For she has grown up with thy empire, noted
Thy reign, if not the wisest, greatest king,
That e'er has reigned o'er mortal Argolis!
   King. But such my wisdom and maturity
This newborn son would be a king from birth,
A born king, not of blood alone, but greatness.
   Apollo. O once great king, thou hast my pity. But

This only. Pity's to the weak, the helpless.
So, hence, unreasoning king, and by thy holy
Fireside, away from thrones and petty kingdoms.
Weigh all thy folly, and prepare to die
In glory as thy coronation, proudly,
Grandly, majestically!
    King.   O Apollo!
    Apollo. For now does Argos love her greatest king,
Because thou art her greatest king. Tomorrow
Thou wilt commit the act to all undo
This glory. Argolis does love thee now,
Does love thy wife. And Danae they have chosen
Queen regent to the throne of Argolis!
    King. O! drive me mad! Destroy me! Dub me fool!
Yea, spurn me, curse me, stab! But never, never,
Call Danae queen! Sith, ere I die, a son
Shall come among my people, there to reign
As King of Argos, wiser than his father,
And grander, nobler, with a stature vast
As great Apollo's self.
    Apollo.   I pity thee,
And I deplore thee. For, O man! O king!
The hour draws nigh when thou shalt find a wonder
In Argolis. Thy very home. Thy throne
Shall shake, for Fate pursues thee like a sin
Descended from thy fathers.
    King.   Speak Apollo!
For I this day have come to thee that Delia,
My wife, my queen, may bear me such a son
As time, and Argolis, and all the world,
Shall call a King of kings. Wilt aid me, Phœbus?
Else do I perish in despair, seek death
E'en at the cannon's front. Go down in gloom
Unto a nameless grave. For else a son
Be born to me, no footstone mark my grave,
No sculptured slab emblazon my proud deeds
As King of Argolis: but nameless, nameless,
Be old Acrisius's memory! So, proud god,
Listen to me! O hear my piteous word.
Wilt call divinity from the skies in aid
Of me, that Delia, my true wife, may be
A second mother, and her offspring live
A breathing, kingly boy? Upon my knees
I do implore it! Kings that bend the knee
Should win propitious favor.
    Apollo.   Does a fool
Go babbling in the land? Has court clown lost
His way, and mimics at a star-god's throne?
Arise, weak man! A coward king to bend
The knee to less than God. Up, up, O man!
Ere lightnings flash and rend thee, thunders roll
In volumed cannonade to shake the pillars
That do uphold thy kingly palace. For,
Dost hear me? Delia's past her pregnancy!
And even otherwise, the child would be

A fool! For thou art in thy frosty dotage.
You prattle like a child; a toothless woman
In old decay. Stand back, thy head erect,
Once more to try to be thy former self.
But, no Dost fawn and babble. Once proud mouth
Hangs listlessly; thy eyes have lost their lustre:
A foolish old-man king does stand before me.
   King.   O mercy, Phœbus!
   Apollo.   Mercy? Didst thy Delia
Find mercy? Back, once king and gloried ruler,
And hear a god's decree. Thou 'lt never be
A father!
   King.   God forbid!
   Apollo.   God will forbid!
   King. I perish on my servant's sword! I die.
   Apollo. Die? Yea! For fate has so decreed it. I
Apollo, throned in clouds and changeless never,
Do now announce thou 'lt ne'er become a father,
But queenly Danæ shalt soon bear a son,
By whose strong hand, Acrisius, thou shalt die!
   King. And he will slay me?
   Apollo.   Yes.
   King.   My daughter's son?
   Apollo. As sure as moons do rise and suns do set.
   King. Then vengeance, vengeance, e'er it be too late!
But, god of earth and thronèd skies, O hear me!
By all that 's grand and glorious in old Argos,
Uprear for me a king! A worthy son.
By all the majesty of Epidaurus,
Trœzene and my principalities,
Grant old Acrisius this. For never glory
To match the glory of the King of Argos.
   Apollo. Thy reign has been a rare and perfect one.
   King. My Danæ 's well equipped to mount the throne:
But such a king as I, may have a wish.
   Apollo. Wishes are but the foolishness of kingdoms.
   King. Adelia 'll have her reign the one great queen
Of Argolis; and yet she bendeth to
My will. And so, propitious god, Apollo,
Have charity. Men may have their base ambitions,
Kings seldom.
   Apollo.   But thy Danæ 's fair as stars
That shone on Peloponnesian plain. She 's
A jewel set in rubies in the crown
Of Argolis, and there she 'll shine for thee
With heaven's eternal lustre.
   King.   But, Apollo,
Though she 's a jewel of first magnitude
I will to have a son!
   Apollo.   Thy will 's thy master.
Go hence and sleep thy sleep of vanity,
And as the draperied folds of golden curtains
Do flaunt and float about thee, sleep and dream,
And then awake, and then behold the empty
Ambition of a Grecian king!

King.   Great Pean!
My malediction on the King of gods,
Old Zeus, and all lesser down to thee;
For, by the grandeur that is mine, and by
The glory of the throne of Argolis,
I swear a son shalt, god! be born to me,
Or Danæ and the throne of Argolis
Shall go to utter ruin, ruin, ruin!
    Enter Ghost.
    Ghost. Thou shalt not only die a soulless king,
But Danæ's unborn Perseus shall slay thee
With winged discus!
    King.   Heavens, 'tis Danæ's ghost!
                      [*He staggers back.*
                Curtain falls.

ACT II.

SCENE I.

Acrisius in the Palace Garden.

  King. Great God! to thee I lift my humble voice
For mediation in behalf of me
And mine. But, bah! A fool to raise my face
To one so far in space, and little caring
For kings, mere kings. 'T is I, old Argolis,
Acrisius, king of kings, where highest effort
Must quick ensue. Who stronger than a king?
And such a king as I? Apollo, god!
I do defy thee! Phœbus, I do swear it
By all the skies above me, rifted clouds,
And space, and time, and earthly sovereignty,
Things human and divine, and so inhuman
As make the blood run cold, and shudders creep
Across the fibrous system, gnawing, gnawing,
Till life itself is torment, and the victim
Begs for that mercy which is death! Ha, death!
No son. No father. Bah! and yet a son!
A wicked instrument in hand of fate
To brain me in the glory of my prestige.
But, mark ye, lords and knights and ladies grand,
And every cursèd thing that breathes, this son
Shall never be! This child-boy ne'er shall taste
The milk of mother's breast, nor hear the voice
That says: O baby mine, thou 'rt fair as Danæ's
Sweet self, and she will cherish thee, and rear thee,
As her brave boy-king of old Argolis.
But this shall never hap. I 'll kill this Danæ,
I 'll drug her cups. I 'll starve her stomach jot
By jot. I 'll prison her where worms do crawl,
Where rats do gnaw, and must and damp and mold,
And carnivals of vermin, stinking dank,
Do hold high festival. I plume myself,
I decorate my personality,
Recrown the noble brow of such a king
As never ancient history found a greater.

Now, hark ye, I'll construct a brazen chamber,
A subterranean dungeon, where new days
Can ask no blessing, ever circling suns
Bid a good morrow. Once behind the bars,
These dungeon bars, where rust will soon encrust them,
I'll bid defiance to the gods, and even
Divinity himself.
   Enter Danæ.
   Danæ.   Good morrow, father;
Why walkst thou here in silence and alone,
With God's blue arch, and the sun-hidden stars
So wondrous o'er thee? With the summer's balm
From thousand myriad flowers, tulips, roses,
Jasmine, anemones and fenced exotics
Converged in one great cornucopia
Of loveliness.
   King.   In sooth, fair Danæ, life's
Buoyant on thousand gales enwafted from
Arcadian Paradises. Thou didst seek,
Thou soughtst the meaning of my present walk.
Children and girls, and even men of crowds,
Do little reck the rioting thoughts that course
Kings' heads. To wear a crown, child, to the throng,
The commonalty, may seem trifling act.
But dost thou know an Atlas mountain weighs
Not heavier than the crown of gold that glitters
Upon the brows of kings? 'Tis thus I walk,
'Tis thus I talk, 'tis thus I meditate,
'Tis thus I find a solace in a yard,
A pasture, a dungeon e'en, so that it be
My mind from empire bondage is set free.
   Danæ. As you are old, I felt—
   King.   Old? Old? Who says it?
I'm in my prime. Maturity is last
To grace the brow of kings and queens. The limbs
May stiffen at the joints. But mind, the mind,
'Tis greatest, grandest, at a man's old age.
But, Danæ, dost thou see the coming weakness
That oft presages sure decline? Look close!
Has lustre vanished from my eye? My face,
Has health left gaunt and old emaciation?
And do I totter in my steps? Am shaky
Like palsied men who hasten to the grave?
Look, Danæ, look! My eye does sparkle now!
My lips are mobile, and my tongue has lost
No pliability. I'm young again!
The very thought puts vigor in my veins.
My arm. We'll dance. My breath is quick as thine.
            Trip lightly, e'en in age,
        And Time will hold his breath,
          Only the old men die
            Who hunting go for death!
   Danæ. Father, thou dost surprise me.
   King.   Danæ, kings
Are mysterious. All their thoughts are not to those

Who read but lightly.   Potent minds may search
The intricacies of the minds of kings.
Look back in old-world history, and thou 'lt read
The lessons of the ages.   Polytheism,
The strange belief in many gods, was ancient
Religion.   Israelites may bear the palm
For purity, simplicity and honor:
But human kings of gods and men have won
A great renown, until the name of king
Has dignity and greatness in the sound.
See: King Acrisius!   Dost thou mind the sound?
Is 't not more potent than to say: A captain,
A general, knight, and e'en a prince?   It 's not
So much the word as meaning that attaches.
For such the work of kings from times unread,
And read, still unremembered such the age,
That king, the word, has greatness in it, greatness.
  Danæ.   Yea, father, and the name but as a name,
Of king, did long ago impress me.
  King.   And
Danæ, if so to thee, how much more so
To vulgar throngs, who never rub against
The vesture of great kings or little?   For
Association breeds a kind of low
Contempt for e'en the highest.   Our religion,
Danæ, believes in many gods; divine
And earthy.   Wild adventures of our gods
Have been the chief delight of Greeks.   Ingenious,
We 've pictured them with skill and forceful arts
Unread in any other nationality.
Our gods are higher than a king, for death
To them is nameless, unavailing, stingless.
  Danæ.   On snow-clad mountains of Olympus reigned
These gods?
  King.   E'en so.   And gates of clouds unclosed
Their valves, to let celestials wing to earth.
In palace of the great Olympian king
They sipped their nectar, ate ambrosia rare.
Old Vulcan made their golden shoes, their houses
Of beaten brass, and chariot cars.   The Euxine
And Mediterranean were their only seas.
But, Danæ, why talk thus?   Why tell of glories
In high Elysium?   Because a king
Is more than these.   Because a king is highest,
Grandest and mightiest of created man.
He 's more than man, sin once the name of king
Has clothed him, he is deified, a—king!
  Danæ.   I know there 's grandeur in the name of king,
That certain noise, eclat, distinction, sound.
Accrue from hearing.
  King.   Right, my Danæ, right!
And never woman since so rare a gift
As thine that seest the greatness of a king.
And may Aurora smile upon thee, child,
And may sweet Zephyrus waft nectar sweets

Unto thy nostrils. And bright Helios
Shine on thee as the wife of some great king.
But, Danæ, leave me. Younger men than I
Should have thy time, sith now the hour is nigh
For you to wed some lord of chivalry.

Danæ. I love my mother, and my father e'en
As duteous child. That other love I know not.
But, let me leave thee to those potent thoughts
That suit the heads of kings. [*Ex. Danæ.*

King. Adieu, fair lady.
Indeed a lady born she is, and lovely
As ever Delia in her maiden prime.
But, hark! Can beauty come atween us? I
To stand aside for sure ascension of—
I pause. I hesitate. No, no! I'll hie
Me hence. I'll seek the man that hews the stone,
The great artificer who shapes the brass
To sundry shapes and styles, with workmanship
To tease the souls of mister artisans. So,
Adieu to all my principles, my love
For Danæ, all her virtues and unsullied
Beauty. For fame is more to me than love,
Is more to me than glittering gold, and rubies.
If Delia die, then what's to reck? She's past
Earth usefulness, and lives in glories gone,
In evanescent glamor and the hue
And cry of thrones. I'll hence, for ruffian hands
Must tear this daughter from her home, and thrust
Her through the roof of this, her brazen chamber;
Sith it shall have nor door nor crack nor window.
Save guarded aperture upon the apex,
Down which hard villian hands shall lower her;
And once my lady prisoner entombed,
The end will soon develop, so that I
Can strut the streets of Argolis unhampered;
For never lover hath her secret, never
A god can trespass till slow death hast made
My child more beautiful in that last sleep
From whence nor god nor man nor woman fair,
Hast e'er returned, or sent a message back. [*Ex. king.*

SCENE II.

The Palace garden. Enter Danæ and mother.

Danæ. But he has gone, my mother. Not a moment
Hardly, and he went stalking up and down
In loud-mouthed talk with such accompanying manner
As struck me with a nameless fear, a dread
Unborrowed, that some newer kingly trouble
Did rack his brain.

Queen. Come sit beside me, Danæ.
And list my tale. Thy father's blood is boiling,
Fermenting, that he has no matchless son
To wear his crown when he shall fall at last
A clot of earth, a less than man, a mocking
Disfigurement of clay, the soul escaped

At last to where?
 Danæ.   O, mother! hesitate,
For we are not the judges e'en of kings.
 Queen. Nay, Danæ, nay, we must not dare to judge;
It is a fearful thing. But, daughter, child,
The king is strange. He dreams aloud. He revels
Like drunken man in nighttime, and he tells
Of dungeons, chambers brazen, shining brass,
Slow creeping death, a beauteous maid, a boy,
A babe, a son, and her son! Canst thou read?
For dreams are truth, the honest revelations
Of human minds unguarded.
 Danæ.   Mother, I
Can justly apprehend a new affliction.
O spare the word, but has he as a king
Committed deeds that might appeal to heaven?
 Queen. O durst not ask me! He is what he is.
 Danæ. I read. He has been turned from strictest honor.
But let it lie entombed. My cue's this conduct.
 Queen. Oh do not borrow trouble, trouble, trouble;
He's Hydra-headed, many-mouthed, and wicked,
And waits upon the new-made bride, the bridegroom,
The crowing babe. He mouths at every window;
But, fears. You have them?
 Danæ.   Aye, indeed.
 Queen.   But list,
He rages now. But soon 't will pass, I reck.
 Danæ. Mother, 't was once I bragged that I was born
A girl, wore comeliness and native beauty;
I looked to heaven with soft appealing eye;
In mild approval and great thankfulness
I honored God for it!
 Queen.   You pause. You bow.
What means this transient mood? For transitory
Such moods must be. Sith Danæ's envied by
The whole great kingdom of old Argolis,
That she's the king's one daughter, and the heiress
Direct to his great throne. And yea, the damsels
Of mere artificers too, and mechanic
Man are today in envy of thyself.
 Danæ. Poor damsels! Yet they cannot know. A maid
Anear a throne may seem personified
To something finer, more idealized
Than she that milks her father's kine. But, mother,
God only knows how bitter and portentous
The menacing fate of Danæ.
 Queen.   Do forbear
This wicked mood. For he, the King of Argos,
Has only me in web of discontent.
 Danæ. O that 't were so. But, no. For should it hap
That great Apollo still deny his hest,
And you do fail in life's first art, the birth
Of one sweet child, his rage will repercuss,
And then rebound against his only daughter.
 Queen. That this may never hap. And yet, my Danæ,

Let's pray for that divinest intercession
Only the one great God can give.
    Danæ.   Yes, mother.
    Queen. Now let me lead thee forth where Peace is smiling,
Where joys are still atilt, and tiptoe Capid
Does stand awaiting. Come, for woe is here,
And petty strife for fame that has no reason
Only in wicked mind of him who bares it.
    Danæ. My father, king and proud, of Argolis.
    Queen. Thou 'rt fair as Eos. To Hesperides
I 'd take thee ere too late.
    Danæ.   But kings are just.
    Queen. When justice does redound to them, their glory;
But Erebus pursues thee in the person
Of old Acrisius, once worshipping father.
    Danæ. But you more nearly try him.
    Queen.   I 've no no;
But, failing I, his wrath may turn to thee,
A sort of nightly Momus. But, O grant
That I may bear this son; for though it lose
The throne to Danæ, 't will protect her life,
And Melian nymphs shall pipe a newer song
To beauty unrewarded and great worth.
    Danæ. I hope this accusation is at fault;
But though a Venus or a bright Electra,
I 'd weep soft Iris tears ere I 'd ascend
The throne of Argolis against his will.
    Queen. Well said, and nobly. Fair Ionian Greeks
Will honor thee, and some new Cimon love thee,
And ocean nymphs from grotto palaces
Shall rise on new glad waves to welcome thee.
    Danæ. Mother mine, thou dost seem a fair Selena
In all thy mother kindliness to me,
For God's great moon is calmness beautified.
But, let 's away to life's serener fields,
And let good morrows build their fates for us.
                            [*Ex. Queen and Danæ.*
    Enter Acrisius.
    King. Ye powers of hell and all satanic regions,
I 've done it! His infernal majesty
Has set my head agoing till my brain
Has builded such an architectural structure
That Satan cannot enter. Hundred servants
Stand waiting to my call. But, King of Argos,
Trust now no man. Be now thyself thy servant,
A hair, and thou thyself wilt fill this chamber!
Felldaff the brazier, I will hie to. He
Shall build this brazen tomb for living corpses,
Since, hark ye, Danæ and her blubbe'ly nurse
Shall hence where trite Omega crowns the dome.   [*Ex. King.*
    Enter two villains, Hardspur and Brasker.
    Hardspur. Where went he, Brasker?
    Brasker. Just through the grove, Sir Hardspur.
    Hardspur. King or prince, his money 's ours.
    Brasker. For we need money more than bread.

Hardspur. Since without money without bread.

Brasker. But, come. What matters it, lord or beggar,
If he have the stuff?

Hardspur. Quick! I follow.   [*They follow with drawn swords.*
Enter Acrisius, followed by Brasker and Hardspur.

King. Now will I forth to quiz old Felldaff. He 's
As cunning as a woman, and can build
His brasses with divinest inspiration.
The figured beast or brazen slab is his;
The couchant lion 's transfigured by his art,
He 'll turn the brooklet into hewèd brass,
With waving tree and intersecting flower,
Until, egad! you 'd envy him his glory.

Hardspur. And his brasses will outlast the fame of kings.

Brasker. And stand in monumental memory when
The kings of Argolis are forgot.

King. Ho, ho! What common men are these? Aside!

Hardspur. This is gentleman Brasker, yclept villain.
At your services.

Brasker. An' this, me lord, is Hardspur, rogue
At large, his appetite always in his stomach.

Hardspur. And where should it be?

King. Forsooth! A worthy couple. May a king—

Hardspur. A—king! He, he!

Brasker. A—king! Ha, ha!

Together. A—king! Ha, ha! A—king! He, he!

King. And dost thou dare intrude upon my presence?

Together. We dare intrude upon thy presence.

King. These jokes be grim with such a mind. Thy reasons?

Together. An appetite 's no joke. We 're hungry as hunger.

King. Then eat, bold sirrahs. The town 's full of bread.

Hardspur. But the baker does guard the bread.

Brasker. And the law does guard the money.

King. Here, take my purse! A king, sirs! cannot dally.

Brasker. A king!

Hardspur. A purse?

Brasker. Thy purse is sick to emaciating consumption.

Hardspur. An' 'sides, no king e'er had such weakling.

King. But I'm the king of Argos. See my signet
Ring? See my diapered emblems, yea! my badges.
And more, I 'm in the boundaries of the garden
Of old Acrisius. But dost dare believe me?

Hardspur. A king!

Brasker. A real king?

Hardspur. We drop on humble knees.

Brasker. For we are sorry we are caught.

King. Arise! Put up thy swords. I 'd have thine ear.

Hardspur. Take Brasker's: 't is larger.

Brasker. His; for 't would make a purse like any sow's.

King. Have done. My head is full of nameless meanings.

Hardspur. My stomach 's full of emptiness, and cries
For mercy.

Brasker. Mine cries for bread.

King. As sure as I am now revealed the King
Of Argos, just so sure will I make you

Both independent. Yea, a few days hence
Thou 'lt come to me. Come armed. Come well prepared,
For blood is in it! Beat the guards, the knights,
But seize fair Danae, old Acrisius's daughter,
Quick bear her to the dungeon quarter, where
In brazen chamber, with her spluttering nurse
You force her. For this wily brazier ten
Short days henceforward will so build the room,
That only hirèd men can find the cunning
Passage. One week and three short days, my men,
And she 'll be ready. You 'll be ready. I 'll
Be ready. Canst thou understand my meanings?

   Hardspur. I understand, he understands.

   Brasker. You want starvation to murder her?

   King. Hush!

   Hardspur. You want her grave dug a little sooner?

   King. Hist!

   Hardspur. We 'll take thy purse and serve thee.

   Brasker. The fatal hour will find us as fatal.

                       [Ex. Hardspur and Brasker.

   King. Now will I on my way to busy Felldaff's,
And have the brazen cage in readiness
For wingless bird. One business is attended,
The villain's part. And it bespoke a business
Trait seldom the equipment of old kings.   *[Ex. king.*

SCENE IV.

In Danae's room. Enter queen.

   Queen. And I have come because I fear with thee
A crime is on the eve of culmination,
Of whatsoever nature I 'll not dare
To tell thee. But, my child, let caution mark thee,
Let moderation lead thy steps. Be calm.
Be placid. Caution may keep villains out,
And moderation so construct thy walks,
Thy movements, that his well-intended snares
Shall find no victim. And be calm and placid;
For calmness and placidity are oft
Great generals ere the action of the troops.
If days can pass ere guessèd plot shall deepen
To wicked culmination, time may change him,
Aye! death engulf him. For he 's old as men
Who do prepare for coming dissolution,
Because they know it. More to God they turn;
They look farewells. Their faces wear the sombre
Hue that presages life's sad end. They make
Their wills, with many a cunning codicil,
And have a sort of hand-to-hand encounter
With death himself.

   Danae.   I mind the stress, the accent,
All wisest actors show in studied parts;
But, mother, language has no human meaning
With application unto him however
Well turned and studied, since thy ill-turned face
Belies it. All thy manner, movements, pose,

Position of thy head: for love has his,
And hate and sorrow. Here the cunning actor
Rises to heights of acting truly great.
    Queen. And so I rank inferior as an artist,
With such a critic as my only daughter?
    Dana. Yes. For the king, my father, has so changed,
That some new language must be sought to hide him:
Sith in these moods he needs another face,
A new expression and a newer manner.
    Queen. Why thinkst thou so?
    Dana.   Because he looks at me
In such a style, I read: Yea, cursed the hour
That saw this child a girl! My kingdom had
She been a boy!
    Queen.   O Dana! spare thy father.
He's in his imbecility. He meaneth
Well.
    Dana. Mother, time alone can show it, time.
    Queen. But, Dana, I do feel the fullness of
Thy meaning, and so feeling, I will hence
That I may soon devise some means, some plans,
To render matters plainer.   [*Ex. Queen.*
    Dana.   Oh to God
That I had been a boy! For then I'd tamed
The Hydra, won my spurs, and been a knight
Of great renown. A prince-knight ready to
The throne, and perfect suited to my father,
With emblems, medals, and accoutrements
Of kingly office, with a belted sword
Ready for quarrels, yet undyed in lurid
Blood. But a girl! A weakly woman fair,
A lily pale that lives for fleeting show.   [*Ex. Dana.*

SCENE V.

Felldaff's shop. Enter Acrisius.

    King. What, ho! thou burly giant with thy smutted
Face, leathern apron, and a visage hard
As adamant, e'en busier than the bee
Of Hybla: dost thou know me, worthy Felldaff?
    Felldaff. I prithee, yes, the noble King of Argos,
The first in peace, and first in justest quarrel,
And, truth, the greatest king since Argolis
Did grow a kingdom.
    King.   Ha, well said, great Felldaff.
And wast thou cunning in thy life as in
Thy work, e'en kings had feared thee, and the hammer
Of merest mechanism were now unknown
To thee.
    Felldaff. Dost flatter me, O King! But why
This interview?
    King.   Of that we'll barter later;
But hear me, kings are less than kings who go
Not 'mong their subjects, there to weigh their wants,
And borrow greatness from the genius of
The populace, the better to adapt

The throne to them, and show that kind of rule
That climes and lands beyond the sea shall say:
The King of Argos goes among his people,
He seeks the brazier, glazier, and the men
Of workaday employments, farmers, carders,
And artisans of every hap and style;
And thus deduces laws, and rules, and codes,
That make his empire second unto none.
   Felldaff. A worthy manner, and Acrisius has
That manner.
   King.   So, we 'll interchange our thought;
And worthy Felldaff, master workman in
Brasses to ornament kings' foot-stones, zinc
And copper to entangle in a fretwork
Of rarest beauty of design, shalt cater
To kingly ignorance, and while an hour
In suave discussion of the common things
Of life.
   Felldaff. I 'm at your services, O King!
   King. Brass, sir, has been and is to be a stable
Commodity. 'T is an alloy of copper
And zinc, and 's used in household furnishings,
As certain parts of fine machinery,
As ornament in much creative art
Devolved from genius. Yellow brass in ancient
History, profane and biblical, has been
To me a theme of wonder. Rare musicians
Employed it in their instruments of melody,
Gates, vessels and a great variety
Of articles had brass in varied forms.
   Felldaff. Thou talkest like master workman.
   King.   I 'm mechanic
Only as king among his books. What church,
What throne, has such a finely rare distinction
Unless the brazen candlesticks be part
Of their equipment? Once inlaid on stone,
Brasses become a lasting monument.
Great kings that were to be commemorated
Stood grandly in imperishable brass.
The foliated cross is still of brass.
Old altar tombs shone out resplendent thus.
The church-way bore on paves these brazen emblems.
Armorial decorations and inscriptions
Were oft of brass, with such a trick of art
As won the admiration of the world.
Huge slabs of brass bore ornamental flower-work,
Rivalling the flowers themselves.
   Felldaff.   Then petty I.
   King. But hist! Thy ear, and yellow gold shall sparkle
Within thy flaccid purse, and rubies rare
Shine in refulgence on the fingers of
Thy wife. For, hark ye, hie thee with a close-shut
Mouth to the dungeon quarter of my castle,
And there a brazen chamber build that hast
No outlet but to heaven. And done, this chamber

Of builded brass, and thou shalt be a king,
A money-king.   For gold shall cross thy palm,
And diamonds glitter on thy workday fingers.
    Felldaff.   The chamber shall be built of slabs of brass,
With aperture so cunningly devised
That only kings can mark it.
    King.   Knight of brass,
Do this, and ne'er will brazen cage contain
A lovelier bird.
    Felldaff.   This work shall be my best.
    King.   And keep thy mouth as close as brass itself
That is the coffin of some pharaoh king:
For, shouldst thou lisp a syllable, bold sirrah!
The gods will be upon thee, and within
This brassy dungeon thou thyself shalt perish,
Aye, inch by inch, and jot by jot, as slow
Vermin do crawl, and time, when watchers wait
For coming death.   Since this is from the throne,
The king himself does usher it.   So, hence
With cunning tool and chisel sharpened fine,
And all accoutrements of craft so deft,
And may the blessing of Apollo crown thee,
And may the gods propitiate thy work,
And all good angels prosper thee, till time
Do crown thy work with rarest consummation.
    Felldaff.   I am nor Vulcan nor a god divine,
With inspiration from the wonder skies,
To build to beauty things of old mechanic
Art.   But, O King!   Mnemosyne as guide
To spoils of other years long buried, I
Felldaff, will build to beauty's rare perfection
A tomb of beaten brass to be the envy
Of kings as yet unborn, and be a brazen
Monument to builder's everlasting fame.
    King.   May Phœbe throw a lustre on thy work:
Asteria, like another milky way;
May Perses shine with new effulgence, Felldaff;
Aurora smile from God's great sky, and I,
E'en greater far than these, reflect my greatness
To this, thy last great masterpiece.
    Felldaff.   I bow,
Yet not as empty men to kings, but for
The wisdom of a man who's more than king.
    King.   'T is nobly said, O king of men!   And may
Some empire great as mine be crowning portion.
For, Felldaff, if a man e'er lived uncrowned
That more deserves it, then the fates are cruel.
But, Felldaff, this grand tomb shall stand to thee
When children yet unborn shall hear the story
Of Argos's greatest king, how he did hire
A noted brazier to erect a tomb
Of brass to place his daughter Danæ in,
Forever to remain, or till the veil
Of death should smother her.   And pilgrims footsore,
Make brave essay to read the brazen dates.

Felldaff. Thou hast a knack of reading times unread.
King. 'T is so. But 't is my greatest hour. To build
A tomb, or build an empire 's now in balance.
If Danaë live, a perishing old kingdom;
If Danaë die, and kingly son be born,
Then such a kingdom as no time has seen.
   Felldaff. And may thy greatest wishes be achieved.
   King. And so they shalt, by all the stars in heaven.   [*Ex. king.*
   Felldaff. Forsooth! And I 'm a tool to use a tool:
And yet a king has willed it, and a king
Is law itself. From kings there 's no appeal.
We commoners bow to the yoke and wear it
With seeming grace, and do congratulate
Ourselves that we are happy in a kingdom
Of lavish laws, and purposes, and tenets,
Not thinking that a wiser way could be,
Or better modes of government prevail.
O happy ignorance of every throng;
We know to work, to strive, to build, to make,
To love, to woo, to wed, to raise, to rear;
But, a great king has trespassed here. His word
Is law to me. I have no other route;
So, I will hence and build this brazen tomb.
   Enter Hardspur and Brasker.
   Hardspur. Now at him, Brasker, with thy glittering sword; sith
If we 're to turn murderers we 'll commence on this workaday lubber.
   Brasker. Stand on the other side, Hardspur, to catch my sword
As I run it through him.
   Felldaff. But, gentlemen, are you crazy?
   Hardspur. Do n't let the word gentlemen befool us. Run him
Through, my brave Brasker.
Felldaff. Help, help!
   Hardspur. Now at him, Brasker.
   Brasker. Stick out your belly. There! I 've done it. Hardspur,
Look upon an uncrowned hero, Sir Brasker!
   Hardspur. Let the curtain fall. 'T is a climax.
   Brasker. And we are murderers.
   Hardspur. You!   [*Pointing his index finger at Brasker.*
          Curtain falls.

ACT III.

SCENE I.

Zeus, the King of gods on Mount Olympus.

   Zeus. How had the great world moved had Rhea, mother,
And Saturn, father, not united? I
Was babe of that connection, now the king
Of gods and men. But, 'spite this hap, O World!
I, Zeus, had not tasted length of life,
Had not this mother, wiser than a king,
Concealed me in a dark cave of Mount Ida,
In Crete, where Hybla bees and doves did feed me,
And all good gods attended, Amalthea
Furnishing her precious milk of life. But now,
O wrinkled earth in all thy hoary years,

Thou findst me not the swaddling babe of tears,
But Jupiter giant, with a power to shake
This great Olympian throne, go thundering down
The centuries untold, with consummation
Of old earth glory, as shalt last as long
As time himself. The thunder is my weapon,
Ægis invulnerable shield, that Vulcan
So builded howling storms and tempests come
At potent bidding. The majestic eagle
Is yet my favorite bird. Of trees, the oak,
Growing upon the everlasting hills,
And master of the storms and time himself,
Is sacred. He's a king. I only am
Greater. I am the national god of Greece,
Greece with a glory as the setting sun,
Her Doric art the admiration of
The world. Her old Ionic architecture
Descended from Assyrian lands to be
Perfected by the Grecian knight of plumb,
And line, and level. Where is any land
To match old Greece's pure Corinthian art?
Our marble Caryatides modelled from
The loveliest female figures of all Greece?
And where's the land to boast a lovelier woman?
Our Doric, copied from the wooden huts
Of aborigines, is perfect Greek,
And our Ionic, with its fine volutes,
Is classic, our Callimachus with wings
Of inspiration soaring to the skies!
But, Greece, with all indebtedness to Egypt,
And old Assyria, what art is such art
As human forms divine? A perfect man!
A perfect woman! Greece, thou hast these rivals:
And yet the marbles of thy classic land
Are perfect imitations, and are glorious.
But in the midst of all this human beauty,
And in the midst of all this sculptured art,
I hear of one, a lady fair, who shines
As Venus star, and is the only daughter
Of a great king, the king of Argolis.
Her name is Danae, and by all the gods
Of earth and sky, and angels winged in space,
She shall be mine! I'd wed her for her beauty,
And all her loyal notoriety.
Nor lord nor lover nor the king himself,
Defy me. Now, Olympus, will I go
To Argos on this high acropolis,
And fetch a bride to thee to be thy queen,
And beauty's ruler till the world shall fall.   [*Ex. Zeus.*

SCENE II.

In the dungeon quarter. Enter Felldaff.

Felldaff. I'm but a tinker in the land of Hellas,
For only tinkers do the bidding of
A pirate lord. But here am I, the master

Of Grecian brasses, turning all my art
To basest end. For though I said it not,
Yet Felldaff smells a fine malaria
In King Acrisius's kingly disposition.
The king's in trouble. 'T is a human something
That vexes him, insures his sovereign choler,
Or else this brazen chamber had not been.
I'm in my native country, in a land
Of freedom, art and literature, of song,
Philosophy, and genius for all greatness.
The Adriatic, and Ceraunian range
Of mountains are our boast, and old Olympus,
With king of gods. And yet is money my
True god. I may admire Cambunian ridges,
The great Ægean sea, and Mediterranean,
Ionian waters leaping into song;
But gold 's my god. The king will tap his mine.
The Gulf of Arta, or the Gulf of Volo,
May still entrance me. Yet, O Fame! of thee
Felldaff must sing another song. And still,
I mind me of the hours and hours I spent
In building Grecian brasses, my creations,
Second to none. The Pindus chain of mountains,
The backbone of old Greece, may now enthrall me,
Dividing Thessaly from old Epirus,
Cape Sunium and Helicon, Hymettus,
And rugged Pass of famed Thermopylæ,
May have a kind of inspiration; yet
O Fame! and yet, O earthly Glory! I,
Felldaff, must woo the mammon of the world.
So will I build this glowing chamber, tomb,
And keep the tongue of Felldaff from its wagging.
This tomb may be my own brass mausoleum.
But King Acrisius has decreed. A brazier,
No word. So, now adieu, dear fame and art,
I go to build a tomb for some lone heart. *[Ex. Felldaff.*

SCENE III.

The King in his bedchamber alone.

King. Good Felldaff is at work. I hear his hammer.
Now will I curb my temper and await
Expected hour that sees my Danaë bird
Encaged in walls of brass, with single nurse
To tease the hours away, till such an hour
As time shall build from bitter days to come,
And Argos shall not have an inkling. Kings
Can keep a secret, else how blank the history
Of kingdoms, in the eye of day. Am I
Not wise as any? I can hold a secret,
For am I not as one that 's versed in lore?
In language? Every male heir to a throne
Is reared and bred and tutored, till he lives
A monument of scholarship. Not only
Was great Acrisius taught his Greece, but Rome,
Italy, the world. Of architecture, Doric,

Ionian, and Corinthian.   What beauty
Did that grand temple at old Corinth boast
In Doric loveliness!   Old Beni-Hassan
Tombs being models.   Grandest architraves
Stretching from pier to pier in airy tracery,
Suggesting dentils and modillions of
The cornice, Polygon and fluted shaft,
Fulfilling all their magic parts.   But why
Durst I dare prate of earth's acquired wisdom,
When, ah! a tomb is building for a queen?
And yet I dare be boastful.   Yet I dare
Be proud of letters.   Oft in fine review,
I've wandered o'er the field of great inventions.
The temple grand of Theseus.   At Athens,
With greater Parthenon, and Jupiter's
At old Olympia, and Apollo's at
Bassæ, Minerva's too at Sunium,
All in the glowing age of old Acrisius!
But, hark!   The brazier's hammer plays a song!
It draws me from my reverie.   Its music
Is mightier than the music of our churches,
Our theatres, in tetrachords of sound.
But I will hie me to this Felldaff brazier.
He'll prate to me of Grecian art and worth,
And how old Argos kings did find their birth.   [*Ex. king.*

SCENE IV.

In the dungeon quarter.   Felldaff at work.

Felldaff.   O brazen tomb, 'mid all my Grecian brasses,
Thou takst the lead.   As long as old Alpheius
Flows from Arcadian latitudes through Elis,
So long this brass shalt stand.   Thy waters too,
May mingle with Ionian seas and lose
Their song, and still this pyramid will be
Eternal to the brazier of old Argos.
E'en time may chase his fame adown the stream
Of death as old Alpheius Arethusa,
And yet shalt brazen monument remain.
Famed Athens, ancient state of Attica,
Shalt perish from old earth and history ere
The work of Felldaff fadeth.   O, Cecropia!
Didst ever hold a like?   Wast one in all
Thy Attic tribes?   Did Theseus hear tell?
O celebrated Gulf of old Saronica!
Did such a Felldaff breathe within thy waters?
Phalerum harbors, didst he here embark?
O five-mile Walls!   O forty Stadia! didst
Thou ever hold the likes?   O Salamis!
O Marathon! with splendid buildings, temples,
And all magnificence, will Felldaff's glory
Be as imperishable as thine?   He comes!
Great king, a brazier's welcome.   I'm as busy
As 't were a monument to Felldaff's memory.
   Enter Acrisius.
   King.   Indeed, and so it shalt be, for 't is work

Of art; and builded for a king is sure
Renown. But, good my Felldaff, time is flying.
Are all thy blows as quick as love in youth?
   Felldaff. Aye; for 't is love, ambition, loyalty;
Love of that work, ambition for that work,
And loyalty to that king of Argolis
Who hath no peer!
   King.   Sir Felldaff, it is said;
And were we prisoned in the palace cellar,
Felldaff should taste my Greco, the fine cipro,
White and black moscada, my Livadia
And rare sultana, with vinification
Perfect as gods' wines.
   Felldaff.   Then the brazen tomb
Should halt, with wine-drunk brazier at his wits.
   King. On Santorin 't is glorious to be winy!
Sweet Malvoisie is found in many lands.
The fine red wine of Zante passes muster,
Achaia smacketh of divinity!
   Felldaff. Thy viticulture knowledge is superb.
E'en now I smack my lips in thirsty gusto
At all thy winy wisdom. Malmsey wine
Has often tickled Felldaff's palate, but—
   King. And hast thou tasted my divine Lepanto?
It is superb. The tongue dost swallow twice.
The vineyards of Megara, dost thou know
The gods do relish this as rarest nectar?
And ancient Thera! Blessings on thee. Aye,
Blessings unnumbered, for the king forgets
His throne, its vesture, and its hard exactions
In dreams with thee. Oh, that a million pipes
Did flow to Argolis!
   Felldaff.   Great king, art tipsy
On muscadine, Vin Santo wine of thought?
Or hast the builded chamber so upfilled thee,
Thy mind dost sway with new-found ecstasy?
   King. I 'm not a king drunk o'er his cups nor swayed
By grapes of Andros, Tino, nor the vats
Of Naxos, for exhilaration does
O'erjoy me, that although no kingly father,
I 'm soon to bury her that is to raise
A son to slay the King of Argos. Bah!
   Felldaff. A son? A father? Is the king deranged?
   King. Forbear the word. I spoke as one in wine.
But, hasten. Time is digging thousand graves.
A thousand tombs are making fast. But till
This queen be once forever tombed, the vintage
Of widest worlds has no appeasement. Taste
Is cloyed. The mind is in a whirl of woe.
   Felldaff. Then will I fly as courier who dost go
On kingly errands.
   King.   And the King of Argos
Will more reward thee than hadst built an arch
Of riven brass to his great memory. [*Ex. king.*
   Felldaff. And were the subject not a coward, Felldaff,

The master brazier, should so build this tomb
That this old bibber king might die tomorrow.
And fill its cavernous depths with empty clay.
But kings do sway the world. Will time dare come
When kings are not, and every man shall have
A voice? But on, my Felldaff, kings are mighty.
 Enter Danæ.
 Danæ. O noted Felldaff, with thy brasses scattered
Throughout old Greece, what wonder hast thou now?
 Felldaff. O queen! my mind is sealed by kingly saw.
My tongue is cloven to my mouth since I
Was delegated to this work.
 Danæ.   Intrusive?
 Felldaff. Not more intrusive than a star, a flower,
A potted lily innocent as thou.
But, daughter of a king, and fair as Venus,
If not thyself a Venus, in my honor
I'm not to say my thought.
 Danæ.   Then I've intruded?
But honor unto thee for honor thine,
And mayst thou win new laurels in the realm
Of brass creations.
 Felldaff.   No offence, dear lady:
And Felldaff thanks thee for this happy kindness,
Since though the world, its people, and the realm
Of Greece do know and honor me, 't is seldom
A very queen descends to deign me homage,
Or cast a glance at such creations. For,
Dear lady, and so fair, most kingdom adjuncts
Are busied more with life's new passing fashions,
The petty gewgaws of time's passing styles,
The evanescent, fleeting follies of
A day. 'T is thus a brazier's great conceptions,
Or Phidian sculptures, built in imitative
Art of mere passing styles of human dress,
Do seem like ancient furniture. But he
Who sculptures to the life, the nude in art,
Has everlasting monuments to his
Great memory. For does nature find no change,
But styles, I trow, do change like ladies' minds.
 Danæ. Thy soft impeachment is so couched in wit,
And climaxes so all thy feast of praise,
That Danæ says amen to all thy wordy
Wisdom.
 Felldaff. But some do say that thrones alone
Possess all wisdom.
 Danæ.   Felldaff, bite thy tongue
For such estrangement of the truth. The king
Is but a human being. Wisdom 's given
To few. An education may develop;
And yet how oft we hear of Felldaff greatness
Beneath the shadows of old thrones. Too much
Assistance and does genius pale and wane.
 Enter queen.
 Queen. And so I've found thee, Danæ?

Danæ.   Yes, my mother.
Queen. And watching worthy Felldaff in creative
Art? Only finest senses have the trait
That loves these things; sith art for art alone
Is high achievement, and dost e'er outsoar
The vulgar mind.
Felldaff.   Indeed, queen lady; but
True fame to such as I, is 'yond the portal.
Death.
Queen. Haply for a few, but Felldaff, never.
Already Grecian bards have sung thee. Time
Too has crowned thee more than king, for kings
Do die, with no memorial to their glory,
While Felldaff's live forever in their art.
But, famous Felldaff, sir, what hast thou here?
These slabs of polished brass. What mean they? They
Do look as cold as death. A very tomb
They do appear. Dost pause? Thy head is hung.
O Danæ! my true child-queen, I can reck
'T is crowned Acrisius's brazen tomb, his tomb
Of nightly dreams, and near the dungeon quarter.
Danæ. Sir Felldaff's honest as the day. His hand
Has never shaped unworthy thought. He loves
His art, and generations yet unborn
Will say: The ancient brazier, Felldaff, never
Builded his brasses unto prurient minds:
But everything in loftiest conception.
Felldaff. [*Aside.*] May palsy seize me if I dare dishonor
The name of Felldaff!
Queen.   Thou wast speaking, Felldaff.
Felldaff. Indeed. But common braziers, queen, are best
Unheard, and in their proper places.
Danæ.   I 'm
Sure Felldaff's words have been of sense. But, mother,
We tarry.
Queen. Yes; we will away, for I
Do feel a strangeness in this dungeon place,
Which soon will wear away in other scenes.
So, come, my Danæ, for the king is moody.
Danæ. 'T is nothing new. But his strange meditation
Has grown upon him, till I know not father
As noble king of Argolis. And 'sides,
A dread is creeping over me of times
Not distant, when new troubles will attend.
Queen. We 'll hence, and pray for better dispensations.
Danæ. And lend thy arm. I feel a faintness coming.
Queen. Good child, the ways of kingdoms are a riddle,
Glitter and glare and pompous show and baubles,
Make up the sum of kingdoms. Come. We 'll think
Of common people, and the hallowed beauty
Of cottage homes. I 'm sick of kingdoms.
Danæ.   I,
Too, mother; and I 'd change my lot with maid
Of lowlier worth; for thrones are happy only
In seeming.

Queen.   Come. As Youth and Age we 'll wander,
Finding a kind of solace in communion.

Ex. Danæ and Queen.

Felldaff.   And so a kingdom 's not a Paradise;
And so a throne is not a bed of roses.
So, look ye, worthy Felldaff, thou 'st the fame,
And thou 'st the happiness. In fine, thou art
A king thyself, a very king. The tomb,
The brazen grave today of some unknown,
Is verging on completion. Master strokes
A hundredfold and thou hast done thy work!

Enter Brasker and Hardspur.

Brasker.   Ho, ho, Felldaff! Thought we killed you.
Hardspur.   Ha, ha, Felldaff! Sir Brasker tried to kill you.
Felldaff.   Brasker and Hardspur, my would-be murderers!
Together.   Aye, aye, Lord Felldaff.
Felldaff.   And why a lord, oh spurred and booted rowdies?
Brasker.   Thy wit is grim as brazen tomb thou buildest.
Felldaff.   A brazen tomb? What necromacy 's this?
Hardspur.   It is the wisdom of a lord of fame,
Who dares to sink his art for hireling's pay.
Brasker.   Because, ma foi! a king has bidden it.
Felldaff.   What cowards these to read the future world?
Brasker.   All three cowards. Hardspur, my friend in trespasses, Felldaff, a double-minded man, who turns from his immortal fame in Greece's noblest brasses, to build a hireling's tomb for queenly innocence because a wicked king has decreed it, and Brasker, because he 's a villian because he 's poor.
Hardspur.   Ho, ho, thou man famed in two continents,
Art thou trembling?
Brasker.   He trembleth like a wicked aspen.
Felldaff.   Thou mayst be featured like a courtly fool,
But, faith, thou hast the wisdom of a god,
Else who has dared to prate of kingly secrets?
Brasker.   The king himself.
Hardspur.   A very king.
Felldaff.   Thy wisdom doth belie thy addle looks.
'T is coward's part to play an eavesdropper.
Brasker.   But we never dropped beneath the eaves.
Hardspur.   And the drops of the eaves ne'er dropped on us. We got in need of bread. The town had bread, but money was the little requisition. We had neither. So, honest Felldaff, we knew the king had both. We crossed his path. We met his arguments with drawn purse. We drew our swords, and he, Acrisius—
Brasker.   Drew his purse. And that 's not all, great Felldaff. We two handsomest men in Greece, are hired gentlemen to steal daughter Danæ from her mother's arms, and secretly imprison her till she die in Felldaff's funereal sepulchre.
Felldaff.   O that I'd ne'er been born a kingdom's genius,
For then had Felldaff been an honest man.
Brasker.   We do pity thee in humbler language.
Hardspur.   But our crime is triple. We are Greece's
brazen triplets.
Brasker.   For, if not triplets in birth and likeness,
There 's not a jot o' difference in our calling. We 're

All scamps.

Felldaff.   Felldaff cannot retract, else off his head.

Hardspur.   But honor 's more than fame.

Brasker.   And honesty 's more than heads.

Felldaff.   How wicked be the times! Will promised lord
Descend from curling clouds, and teach this world
Virtue and purity, honesty, uprightness?

Together.   Ha, ha.

Felldaff.   A brazier yet may have a soul, and will,
For here 's the last great stroke that makes the brass
A wicked tomb and brazen monument.
'T is done! And help me, heaven, for ne'er again
Shall Felldaff's art be hireling to a king!

Hardspur.   Well said, my newly convert.

Brasker.   Thou 'st more culpable.   We do work for bread.   You
For money.   But, hereafter, good Felldaff can build to
Beauty little wingless Cupids.   With skill unrivalled,
He can shape the brasses of the gods, the good gods.   Little
Brazen angels he can make.   Of shining brass he can
Fashion cherubim and seraphim.

Felldaff.   My work is done.   I go to seek a holier
Companionship, and then will sing and pray
For Hardspur, Brasker, and their likes, for such
Are universal.   All lands have a sprinkling.
So, Brasker, faretheewell.   And worthy Hardspur!   [*Ex. Felldaff.*

Brasker.   Adieu, reformed Felldaff.

Hardspur.   And may you ne'er be tempted for want of bread.

Brasker.   Ha, ha, Hardspur, a fine species of reformation.
His conscience smote him 'cause we trespassed on his secret.

Hardspur.   But we 'll not repent till the hangman trespass on ours.   I
smile at weaklings of such sort.   Give me a pirate, with beard
descending to his lap.   An eye that pierces like a dagger.   The voice
of a roaring lion.   A mien as august as a king's.

Brasker.   And belted sword, and pistol, and ugly knives.   Egad!   I 'd
be a pirate myself had I the king's wherewithal.   For to rove the
seas, sing coarse songs, and be a bravo murderer, is pinnacle of
earthly glory.

Hardspur.   Hark!   Who comes?

Brasker.   The king!   We 'll secrete ourselves behind
These wings and hear a king's unguarded soliloquy.

Enter Acrisius.

King.   Alone?   And Felldaff gone?   What means it?   Ha!
The tomb is builded!   He has done his work.
And such a work as this!   It has the grandeur
Of ancient tombs.   And 't is sublime beyond.
O worthy Felldaff 't is thy masterpiece!
I knight him now, for such his inspiration
In this new work of high creative art,
That never man in any kingdom far
Or near, hast greater right.   And now, O tomb
Of splendid brass!   I bow to thee as one
Who feeleth all the splendor of a purpose
Moulded from thought, and stands a monument
Of glory unto him as rare creator.
Rich ichor flowed within his noble veins,

And goodly wines from clouded thrones. O Felldaff,
Thou 'st greatest in thy wickedness! But, sooth,
Thou hast no blame, nor I, nor Hardspur, Brasker;
For kings must live in their inviolate trusts,
Whoever die, since such the need of kingdoms.
If other, soon the vulgar would ascend
The throne, and so degrade it, that all empires,
However old, would topple to their fall.
Enough. Apollo does decree that I
Shalt never be a father, and decrees
That Danaë shalt become a mother, and
This son of hers shall slay the king of Argos.
But, Danaë. She must find her living tomb!
Hardspur. Sir Brasker. Would they 'd come to me,
For every hurried moment drives me to
The tomb of old Acrisius. Ere too late
This downy bird I 'd sore imprison. For
Even a king may be too late. I fret.
But Danaë's ghostly apparition? Strange!
  Enter Hardspur and Brasker.
And so they 've come to echo of my word.
Good worthies, dost thou find the cage in waiting?
  Together. We do.
  Hardspur. And such a work of art that e'en a king's
Daughter should love to die for such a tomb.
  Brasker. Ay, sir. And we but do the part of friendly
Mediators in stealing this Danaë from so corrupt
And fleeting a world, and place her in this
Brazen and immortal tomb.
  King. The king does well agree with thee. But time
Is raven-footed, and the busy hours
Do chase each other toward death with such
Exactitude, that even kings on thrones
May well be expeditious. So the hour
Demands the utmost urgency. My daughter
Is now within her room. Despite her cries,
Her protestations of new innocency,
That rare equipment of the justest word
In altercations of this sort, do seize her,
And boldly bear her to the dungeon quarter,
And make her happy visitant of Felldaff's
Immortal handiwork in beaten brass.
  Hardspur. And wilt attend in person?
  Brasker. For a kind of eclat will so be lent.
  King. I 'll plant me here beneath her window-stool,
And note the acts of paid subserviency;
And when the deed is done, then wilt the sovereign
Beshrew himself with paltry lucre. Go!
  Hardspur. We do thy bidding as the shadow of a king.
  Brasker. And if she cry this cloak shall hush her.
                      [*Ex. Hardspur and Brasker.*
  King. Ta! what could be more near a guillotine,
Or rack of inquisition than to be
Alone with one's own guilt? But, fah! a life,
The life of merest king is more than hers.

If conscience hold the reins of human self,
Then Danæ lives, and old Acrisius dies.
A palace room can easier spare its queen
Than kingly kingdom its great ruler. So,
The hand of fate does fall, but in that fall
An empire lives. So, Conscience, thou dost err
In this great hap. For kings are more than queens,
And kingdoms more than palace ladies. Ho!
The mad besiegers do their work! She cries.
What, ho! she scapes them, and outstrips the deer! [*Steps aside.*
    Enter Danæ wildly, screaming, the villains in pursuit.
  Danæ. O piteous Father! save me from my friends,
For all my enemies are more outspoken.
Come boldly out, no secret innuendoes,
And stab me with the venomous tongue of slander.
  Hardspur. Ha, thou hast the wings of the wind.
  Brasker. But canst not scape such worthies as Hardspur and I.
  Danæ. O mercy! Mercy!
  Brasker. Come. For golden ducats, polished by kingly
Pockets, await the drama's climax. [*Seizing her.*
  Hardspur. Hold her fast.
  Danæ. O where 's that kingly father who did rear me?
  Hardspur. Silence, lady, or this broidered cloak
Shall smother. [*Throwing it over her head.*
  Brasker. Now will we bear thee to that divinity
The tomb, where villains molest not, and kingly
Fathers hold their peace.
  Hardspur. And here 's thy tagging nurse, Betta; she 'll
Be thy vacillating companion. [*Seizing her.*] And
She dost quack like cottage hens after the birth
Of an egg. But come Time 's impatient, and
Thrones do balance on the result. [*Ex. all four.*
  King. And now does comedy assume that other
Shape, murderous tragedy, and king of Argos
Can sleep that sleep that knows no conscience, and
Has no bald Fear as midnight's dread companion.
So, now, my crowned Apollo, rear this son:
So, now, my still unpregnant wife, weep tears:
So, now, old Argolis, receive again
Thy crowned Acrisius, with a term of reign,
That decade after decade shalt not find
Nor change, nor trembling, nor a human's fear;
For wisest discipline and purpose mighty,
Have now resumed their sway, and time to her
Is naught. Sith clanging bell, nor prattler's voice,
Nor sounds nor hums of time's triumphal march
Shall reach her ear. She 's dead to me, to Delia,
And to herself so far as towns are known,
Or onward sweep of thrones or dynasties.
  Enter queen, excitedly.
  Queen. O husband, quick! For ruffian hands have fouled
The person of our Danæ with a hostile
Touch, borne her off in brutish violence.
Quick! quick! oh valiant king! I faint, I faint!
      [*Faints as king rushes out.*

King. I 'll trounce them hip and thigh and eye and tooth.
                                        [*Ex. king.*

SCENE IV.

At the brass chamber, Hardspur and Brasker holding Danæ and nurse.

Hardspur. Silence, lady, for the fates are 'gin thee.
Brasker. And thou squalling nurse, hush thy babbling,
Or Hardspur 'll marry thee.
Danæ. But I 'm the kingdom's only daughter. Spare!
And good old king Acrisius will reward thee.
I do implore thee, strangers. See, with hands
In supplication clasped I pray thee now
Unhand me. By the love you bear that mother
Who suckled thee, O give me liberty!
Hardspur. But 't is a chamber monumental in
All loveliness. And 's the work of Greece's noblest master.
Danæ. Felldaff!
Hardspur. So, enter quietly, and the good king, thy
Ambitious father, shalt hunt thee at leisure.
Brasker. And you, dear Betta, lovely as a bloated
Dumpling, go thou first, or Hardspur shall marry
Thee for forty year.
Betta. O, oo, oo! I smother. Danæ, the plague on 't!
Danæ. Oh helpless woman! We 'll submit in grace.
Hardspur. Then, Lady Venus, with love's liquid eye, ascend the dainty
    ladder Brasker has brought thee, and descend by other steps within.
    And the bickerings of the world shall not trouble thee. Nor over-
    turning kingdoms.
Danæ. Resistance is so frail a word for woman,
That, Betta, we 'll ascend and enter into
This brazen prison till time do liberate us,
Or, mayhap, death by slow and subtle touch.
Hardspur. There! thy well-fashioned foot is on the
Rung. Do thou mount up, as angel, rung by rung
To heaven. I 'll aid thee.
Brasker. And Betta, an eastern glory, is already in
The audience chamber awaiting thee.
Danæ. Farewell to life and petty kingdoms. I
Go 'yond the reach of human frailty, where
Death only cometh. Farethecwell, farewell!
Hardspur. And may the goodly angels watch o'er thee.
There, Brasker, they 're in it.
Brasker. We two be villains.
Hardspur. 'T is an age villainy pays.
Brasker. Her violence has gin way to weeping.
Hardspur. Her beauty should have saved her this.
Brasker. Beauty 's no contestant with money-antagonist.
Hardspur. Or kingly purpose in the scale.
                    Thunder and lightning.
Brasker. The gods save us!
Hardspur. An earthquake!
Brasker. Quick! quick! Flee!
Hardspur. The skies do fall.
Brasker. We perish. I 'm killed.
Enter queen.

Queen. O horror! What means it?
Lightning flashes. Thunders roll. Both attempt to flee, Brasker falling dead, the queen standing as one petrified with horror.
Curtain falls.

ACT IV.

SCENE I.

In the dungeon quarter. Enter Zeus, finding Hardspur and Brasker on the floor, the latter dead, the queen having fled.

Zeus. By all the gods of heaven and hell, I'll crack
The earth if such like villainies prevail.
Up, Brasker! Dead? Then well-timed thunderbolt,
With lightning as precursor did its work.
But, ho! Here's master Hardspur. Villain rise!

Hardspur. O King of gods and all God's deeds, I pray,
Beseech thee, spare me as a victim of
Necessity. Else I'd hied to sistine chapel,
And in the earthquake had my pater noster
Well waded through.

Zeus. Oh, craven, when didst lie
However skillful, e'er deceive a god?
Or man? Down on thy knees and quick unravel
This riddle of this Argos king, and quick,
Else oft recurring thunder jar thee from
The earth, and hurl thee to that hot damnation
Thou didst prepare for such an angel, coward!
As God ne'er made before, nor seraphs dreamed of.

Hardspur. I'm wellnigh dead, and parched with fear as never
Man wot of. But, O Zeus! as we walked,
Dead Brasker and my humble self, in palace
Garden, old Hunger so besought our stomachs,
That dire Necessity, mother of my guilt,
Did force us thus to intercept the king,
And with a meaning undeniable
Unto such purpose that the King of Argos
Not only offered bread, but such a purse
As never poor man dreamed of nor a rich.

Zeus. Oh palliate the rogueries of the world.
The guiltless man is yet to come in promised
Lord. But, my wicked cutthroat in the shape
Of human being, so proceed that Zeus,
King of the earth and skies, dost slay thee not.

Hardspur. The purse, god, lined with rubies and the gems
Of oriental kingdoms, was that Brasker
And I should boldly kidnap his one child,
And bear her screaming to the brazen chamber
Sir Brazier Felldaff had prepared at king's
Behest, as he desired a kingly son.

Zeus. And Danae, queen of loveliness, and star
From heavenly lands, stood in the kingdom's highway,
Atween the throne and mad king's loud ambition?

Hardspur. Only a god could guess it. But, O Zeus!
I do repent.

Zeus. As shipwrecked mariner

With waves about his ears and succor gone,
But such repentance 's not of gods. So, hence,
For I would be in better companies.
   Hardspur.   I 'm thankful that my wicked life is spared.
But do thou liberate this Danaë, Zeus,
Ere morning stars fade out before that greater.   [*Ex. Hardspur.*
   Zeus.   A god is more than king. I 'm national god,
And greatest of the gods of Greece. But here 's
A king, a human king, the King of Argos,
Who dares usurp divinity of gods,
And build an empire greater than a god's.
Oh, this be wicked business, and dost smell.
Cronos and Rhea, Hera and Neptunus,
I 'm King of Titans. I 've assumed dominion
Of all the world, and lesser king to ape me?
And now will thrust him as I did the giants
And bold conspiring gods. This Danaë shalt
Become the queenly wife of Zeus. My
Supremacy is wide as earth. Dodona,
Arcadia, Crete thou lov'st me as any,
And more. Thy worship is as high as heaven.
I am the Jupiter of all the Romans,
And Ammon of old Libya. So, Acrisius,
Thou 'lt get thee hence ere Zeus wrath do slay thee.
My titles are as myriad as the stars
That pale in heaven before the splendor of
My coming. Various powers and functions, moral
And physical, have honored seats to me,
And natural, for I 'm law and order, I 'm
Protector of good kings, and gods, and men;
Avenger of all broken oaths, offenses
Too dire for mortal management. I guide
The stars in welkin blue above me. I
Wield yellow lightnings, and ordain the change
Of seasons. Prophecy is mine, great Phœbus
Received his oracle from me. Both weal
And woe I can bestow. So, Danaë, weal,
So, King Acrisius, woe! For great Olympian
Has said it. And Olympic festival
Shall not ensue ere Zeus find his consort.
My amours may be legion with immortals,
Ladies of loveliness; but help me, heaven!
This Danaë maid shall find me pure as Grecian
Wines. Though a god, a truer lover than
A mortal darest boast.   I 'm deified,
I 'm human. I 'm a lover. I 'm a god.
Zeus, king, is celestial as the skies.
Young Phœbus might pursue his Daphne, I
My Danaë. Hark! I hear a human footstep!   [*Steps aside.*
   Enter queen.
   Queen.   The heavenly powers attend me. Here 's a dead man!
A vagabond, if looks do advertise him.
But, O high heaven, god Zeus, and Apollo!
E'en dead men, though they be as high as kings,
Have not the horrid interest that I find

In loss of Danæ. For I've wandered half
O'er Argolis; I've wandered hitherward,
And thitherward: through gardens and old rooms,
Up castle stairs, and down old dungeon steps,
In banquet-hall, administrative court-room,
And audience chamber with its marble busts;
And I did cry out: Danæ, dear, where art thou?
At cellar doors, and: Danæ, art thou dead?
At garden walls, and: Danæ, what's thy hap?
At chamber starred of kings. In high old lofts,
Where musts did smother me. In attics hung
With spiders' intersecting webs. And such
My woman's great temerity that even
A dead man can nor stir nor move me, when
Else, human death in human man had so
Appalled me, I had died in human fright.
But, Danæ, dead or living, thou hast armed me
With superhuman courage; and a purpose
Inflexible as fate. 'But, Danæ! Danæ!
I cry. But, Danæ, Danæ! is the echo.
Yet, hark! didst hear a sound in human tone?
Did dead man in a grim resuscitation,
Regain the voice of life? But, no. He's still.
He's cold. A touch does send a shiver through me,
And had I laid my hand upon the dead
As now, cold death had gulfed me such my fright.
But, Danæ, Danæ, e'en a human stark
In death hast dread nor fear nor tremors cold
At such a silence, such a calm. Nor lash,
Nor eye, nor hand, nor foot its motion. 'T is
The stillness of a corpse that frighteth me.
Ye gods protect me! What do I behold?
Great slabs of brass! Great brazen walls! What mean they?
Nor door, nor outlet. Do I hear a smothered
Cry as from dungeon depths? My ears deceive me.
It is the beating of my heart. O Earth!
Thou art a mausoleum unto me!
With Danæ dead I'll weep myself as dead
As she. For I'm alone so lone without her.   [*Ex. queen.*
     Enter Acrisius.
     King. Delia did make the stars look down and weep,
For such her misery. Ha! she little recked
Her husband, the good king, stood thus so near!
I could but pity her true woman anguish;
But what is grief when kingdoms are at stake?
Is human woe accounted in the scale?
A king should have his kingdom more at heart.
But, let her weep, for tears do ease the soul.
Yet had she felt me near and Danæ nearer,
How had her great heart leaped? How had she rent
The air with burst of joy? But, Conscience, down!
A king should have a harder heart. What's this?
A man? A corse? Ye gods! 't is villain Brasker.
Jove's thunderbolts have riven him. But, faugh!
His work is done. And dead or living, useless!

But thou, O tomb of brass! I do adore thee.
Thou art a monument to brazier Feltdaff,
And glory of a kingdom; for thou mak'st it
Possible for king to live. Born orator,
Oration should be wingèd eloquence,
I crying: Danaë, I did never wander
O'er Argolis, since goodly king had spied thee.
I did not wander thitherward, ha, ha.
Nor hitherward. I did not pace the palace
Garden, outcrying, Danaë. Nor old rooms,
Nor castle stairs, nor down old dungeon steps:
In banquet-hall, administrative court-room,
And audience chamber, with its marble busts,
Crying aloud: O Danaë, dear, where art thou?
Nor cellar doors, with Danaë, art thou dead?
At garden walls and chambers starred of kings;
For, Danaë, every golden second told me
That thou wast here! and by the wisdom of
Thy father. But triumphal time is marching,
Second by second, toward the graves of kings;
So in more comely season and more gracious
Mood I will visit thee. A king's good bye,
And, Danaë, may thy soul find heaven on high.   [*Ex. king.*
   Re-enter Zeus.
Zeus. What villain he and angel she, his wife.
But love of Danaë held my thunderbolts,
Else had I shivered, hip and thigh, his bony
Carcase, and hurled him to the vultures. O'her
Matters involve me. Not the hap of states,
The boom of kingdoms, nor the wider uproar
Of princely doings, nor the carnival
Of office, but new Cupid. He 's my general,
And he shalt scale the high redoubt, and land me
Safely within the brazen tomb of her
I love, sweet Danaë, daughter of a king.
So, while the mother seeketh vainly Danaë,
And villain king delighteth in his horror,
I, King of gods, will woo and win queen Danaë.
                              [*Enters the brazen chamber.*
   Enter Hardspur.
Hardspur. Ha! gods deliver: Zeus-king hath fled,
And I, abusèd Hardspur art returned.
For what? To get the moneys of the king.
The villain moneys for my valorous deed.
And what a villain I? No, doughty hero.
Brasker and I did seize a helpless maid,
With ruffian hand compelled her with her nurse,
To cross the threshold of old death. For never
Again shall her sweet eyes revisit heaven;
Never again shall smiling springtime know her.
And drowsy summer with her million odors,
No more shall offer incense to her nostrils,
Nor paint the verdant field with ravished beauties.
And fall with garnered feasts of spring and summer,
Shall toss his yellow glories all in vain.

And winter cold, with diamond snows and starry
Queen-crowns, shall be to her as vanity:
For she is dead as buried kings of old
Dynasties. But, cist! I hear sepulchral voices.
Art death-dreams of my murdered Brasker? He
Is dead as yellow lightning shafts can make him.
Come, once my lusty friend and boon companion,
And swart accomplice of inhuman deeds,
I 'll drag thee forth and unto thy poor funeral,
As dead cold hero of a brave abduction. [*Removes him.*
They say that dead men tell no tales. So, Brasker,
Even as much as I respected thee
In life, thy death dost fill me with a thousand
Terrors. But these sepulchral tones as from
A subterranean cave, whence come they? Tust!
They 're angel voices in the tomb of Danæ.
O monumental brass of wickedness!
Dost Hardspur dare to liberate thy victim?
The great occasion 's one of eloquence,
And therefore am I stirred by inspiration
To speak the language of the Attic scholar;
But Attic scholarship will ne'er release her.
A coward all my days and petty thief,
I 'll now so honor self, that hoary time,
And life's recording angel shall forget
The horrid deeds agone, and raise his brasses
Unto the virtuous memory of Sir Hardspur.
So, Danæ, and Acrisius's hapless victim,
I come to be thy new Leander. Zeus,
I 'd now defy the gods of Greece for one
So fair. Queen Delia, I will twine a garland
For thee, and soon festoon two severed hearts.
Acrisius, wicked in thy kingly dotage,
I do defy thee and thy gold; for Danæ
Shalt have her freedom. Conscience, thou 'st returned.
I bid good morrow, thou art such a stranger.
I knew thee when a child, and mother Hardspur
Did tell me heaven was near. But she is dead,
And with her thou did-t die, but resurrected,
Thou hast the same old face of innocence.
But, Danæ, Hardspur mounts the ladder. Rung
On rung with Conscience I will climb, till kings
May turn them back, and hold their breaths in trembling.
What, ho! My eyes deceive me! Else the King
Of gods be 'st fastened in this brazen tomb,
And Danæ bends her ear as love did tip
With honey-word his tongue. The devils! Zeus
Has spied me! Now my legs hast thou forgot
Thy speed when justice late pursued thee? Off,
Or riven thunderbolts shall strike thee dead!
                              [*Tumbles down and flees.*

    Zeus appears at apex of tomb.
    Zeus. Great Jove! Did mortal dare intrude? A silence
As tomb of death dost now encompass me.
Can god as I be thus deceived? "T was wind,

The wheels of time in swerveless revolutions,
Or busy death, with sixty funerals to
The hour. Or hum of weddings busier than
Death. Danaë, come thou forth. Not less than gods
Do dare assist thee. Mount the mortal ladder,
And come as one that 's resurrected.
    Danaë.   Zeus,
Great god of heaven and earth, I do thy bidding,
For freedom 's dear as new remembered love.
    Zeus. Divinest love of Jupiter Olympus?
    Danaë. Yea, god-lover. But thou dost do a wrong
In wooing mortal maid whose life is bounded
By death.
    Zeus.   But, lady, my divinity
Is off. I woo but as a mortal lover,
And Perseus shall be golden ornament
Of Danaë's and god Zeus's marriage. So,
Dare sit beside me in my thronèd garments,
And hear the mortal love of mortal man.
    Danaë. But such divinity as thine, O Zeus!
Cannot be shifted as a broidered coat,
Sith heaven's divinity doth cling like love:
Once on, the old earth nature disappears.
And gods are gods despite their other nature.
    Zeus And yet I love as god. On old Pandean
Pipes ditties of sweet loves I 'll play, for thou
Shalt be my human dale-nymph fair as spring.
I 'll be thy Bacchus with new wines of love;
A rapt Adonis to his Venus fair;
As lovely as Narcissus in the story:
No earthly love shall woo as well as I;
No earthly maid, e'en fair as art my Danaë,
Shalt have a love more born of heaven. So, sit
E'en closer. Love is cold without thee, Danaë.
    Danaë. Yet mine is but an earthly love, O Zeus!
And I am only Danae, daughter of
An earthly king, the goodly king of Argos.
    Zeus. And yet thou art divine.
    Danaë.   Through love's blind glasses.
But list, O high Olympian god, thou art
The deity of Olympus. Thou, too, art
The god of rosy skies that span above us,
And for the asking youthful Hebe 's thine;
And Thea, Themis, Phœbe and fair Tethys:
A nod from thee and bright Electra comes;
And Iris, with her dewy freshness, while
I, Danaë, art for thee no just companion.
    Zeus. But thou dost rival all in love's eyes, Danaë.
Asteria, starry as the midnight skies,
Aurora, bright as any fulgent morning,
Vesta and Juno, Ceres and wise Metis,
Are naught with thee in rosy Cupid's balance.
    Danaë. But I have read of gods and queens of air,
Prometheus with the heavenly fire, Orion,
Whom Dawn did steal from earth for mortal love,

Until Orion fell. And Helius,
The fiery sun-god. Circe, the enchantress,
And, king, thy own empowered Hecate!
  Zeus.   Jealous?
Then do I thank thee, for by this true test
Is love first proven. Love that is not jealous,
What is it? Canst my Danæ tell? "T is like,
"T is fancy, 't is a passing whim, a trick
Of mind, that once the lover gone, a newer
Dost fill his place.
  Danæ.   Then do I love thee, Zeus,
Sith by this test thou prov'st it.
  Zeus.   Then, my slave,
Beautiful as Greek that e'er did live. But come,
Thy nurse awaits thy quick return. Once there,
Away from trespass bold, and whispering tongues,
And prowling men, thy Betta dear, will aid thee
In rearing Perseus, thy god-son hero
To be, and King of Argolis unborn!
  Danæ. Then do thou aid me. Love has made me slave,
And till such hour as Zeus king shall say:
I, Danæ, Queen of thy Olympian kingdom,
And wife of its great king, wilt here remain
Till summons comes to call me to my people.
  Zeus. Dear wife, thou art the one true woman pure
Of earth. But come! I lead thee as a lover,
Though Hymen god have made us man and wife.
                              [*Danæ re-enters tomb.*
  Zeus. Now, heaven, now, earth, and all the queens of air,
And gods in starry space, I have a queen
Old earth has never seen since time began.
A few short months a hero shall be born
To sway the destinies of rotten kingdoms.   [*Ex. Zeus.*

                    SCENE II.

Enter queen, weeping.

  Queen. I live, but 't is a living death. The king
Is old and chatters in his talk. He mumbles
Of vaults, of brazen sepulchres, tombed Danæs:
And yet he never finds her, never seeks her,
And when I ask him where is daughter Danæ,
Evasive answers, couched in bitterness,
Do greet me. Then he wanders by himself
As he would be alone, his wife intrusive.
Enter king.
  King. By all that 's foul and festered unto death;
By all the mouldering bones of dead old kings:
By all the rotting corses of great knights,
And courtiers, soldiers, hirelings and the mob,
I 'm wroth as furies, wroth to desperation,
Aroused to ocean tempests, and the snarl
And whirl and wickedness of old damnation:
For I do smell a plot and treachery,
And foulness, murder e'en if plot require it.
And dreams do visit me in lustrous night,

And when Latona's inky blackness palls
The whole cursed world, and e'en in daytime, nighttime,
If, once I drop my head in courted sleep.
I 've heard it whispered, I am addle-pated,
That once I was a king of kings, but old.
I 'm imbecile and witless and do chatter,
And babble, mime and gape and ape and stare;
But 't is that I am mad, in wrath, in temper,
That things do go awry, by contraries.
When all my kingly life, the haps of state,
The ponderosity of empires were
To me mere whims, mere nothings, that a stroke
Of kingly pen did settle. But the heavens!
Now is the kingdom wrong, and signs do show
That point to King Acrisius's overthrow!
    Queen. Good king!—
    King. Good king? Who dares to curse me thus?
Ah, Delia, good my wife, and born a queen,
Affairs of state, and laws disjointed, have
So disarranged me, that my strange excitement
Did bear the semblance of a kingly anger.
But, Delia, what dost trouble thee? These tears?
Is Danæ yet thy melancholy theme?
    Queen. Yes, kingly husband, but I find her not.
    King. But hast thou searched?
    Queen. As any world detective.
    King. Did'st visit since this musky palace well?
    Queen. Ay. And in vain. The slimy toads did greet me.
    King. I 'd wandered half o'er Greece by this late time.
    Queen. And I. But hitherward and thitherward,
In cellars grim, and musty loft; in old
Back yards, and up and down till people wonder
If Delia 's mad. But, look! This brazen tomb!
These slabs of brass! What may they mean, O King?
    King. A whim, Adelia. 'T is the work of Felldaff;
For he 's ambitious as a king. But, come,
Thy face is pale. Good health is more than brass,
Than brazen tombs—
    Queen. But I 've not hanted there!
My Danæ—my—
    King. Mad Delia, come away!   *[Taking her hand.*
'T is cruel thus to wring thy soul. Come, come!
    Queen. I go. I follow. But I faint! O hold me!
             [Faints in his arms, and is carried out.
    Re-enter king.
    King. By all infernal happenings, this Delia
Did wellnigh hamper me. But she 's in swoon,
And while she welters and her slow blood creeps
Again through her old veins, I 'll end this farce.
I 'll bare my arm to foulest deed. I 'll draw
My knife and plunge it to her heart! See, see!
The cold steel glitters! One fell stroke and all
Is o'er. The years are gone since first Apollo
Decreed me fatherless. But, she, Adelia,
My sometimes crazy wife, still wanders hither,

And thither crying: Danae, Danae, Danae!
But lest she find her and o'erturn my kingdom,
I'll end these four years' misery with the knife!
These hired ruffians be the tools of fools.
Today, this hour, I'll end the fatal farce.
Now hush, my heart, sith with upraisèd knife,
A valiant king dost near the brazen tomb
Of one too fair to live, because a kingdom's
At stake. My kingdom's more than human life—
What, ho! I hear a sound! 'Tis childhood's voice.
Ye gods! has Danae maid become a mother?
And given birth to kingly son? If so,
And it turn out Apollo's great prediction,
I'll flay him where he stands, and plunge this dagger
To Betta's heart for treachery, and kill
The trio like to impious gods, and free
My kingdom of its enemies, and all
My nightly dreams of gnomes and fears and dreads,
And once again uprise in kingly prestige,
And sleep the sleep of greatness undisturbed.
I mount the tomb as once I mounted to
The throne of Argolis, and people said:
A king! a king! But Conscience now: A murder!
A murderer! Ho, Betta! And ho, Danae!
Come forth! The king of Argolis commands it.

                               Danae and Betta appear.

  Danae. And didst my noble father call me? That
Father so good, so kind, so all endowed
With great humanity and worldly kindness.
  King. What? Curse the hour that saw thee but a girl!
But look ye, hark ye, I've a query, woman:
What voice heard I? A child's? A boy's? Speak out!
  Danae. 'T was childish prattle of my kingly boy,
A lad four years, and beautiful as gods,
And so resembling thee that men will say:
Behold the grandson of the king of Argos!
A worthy like successor to Acrisius.
  King. But tell me, who's the father of this child?
  Danae. O, spare him! He's the half-god son of Zeus.
  King. Betta, dost thou so tell this trumped-up story?
  Betta. Yes, O King!
  King. Then die at dagger's point for treachery! [*Stabs her.*
  Danae. O good my father, king! O spare him! spare him!
  Betta. I am murdered by a king! [*Dies.*
  King. I've tasted human blood of some base sort,
And as the dagger drips its human drops,
Go thou and fetch the god-boy from the tomb,
Or else I plunge it to the blood-red hilt
In thy fair breast!
  Danae.   Strike, strike! but spare my son!
He's noble. He is good. He's every inch
A king. And he is thy own flesh and blood!
  King. The dagger rises, and 't will fall as fatal,
If thou durst hesitate a jot! Go, go!
  Danae. I go. But plunge the dagger as thou willest,

Only do spare my god-boy, king of kings.

   King. Oh this be dirty business. But a king 's
Aroused. Fell murder 'll be the consummation.
Ha! art as spry as fencer in the ring!

   Danæ. Here 's Perseus, thy own real flesh and blood.

   King. Let go his hand. Come here, thou child of earth
And heaven.

   Danæ.   But spare him. He 's my only child.

   King. Back, back! I say. The gods have said this Perseus
Will kill me if he live.

   Danæ.   But, parent, king,
No blood of mine could do such act. He 's pure.
Release him, and we 'll flee to uttermost
Parts of the farthest kingdoms. And we 'll ne'er
Return.

   Perseus. Mamma, he hurts me.

   King.   Curse the child.

   Danæ. On bended knee I do beseech thee, spare!

   King. Spare? Yea, I will! I 'll spare thee both, and such
A wedding ride as bride ne'er had before,
I 'll guarantee. Ho, Waldruff, art thou deaf?

                     [*Rings a call bell.*

   Waldruff. Here am I.

   King. Now be nimble as an antelope,
And with stout hands to aid thee, fetch that coffer,
That great old coffin-chest. And be thou quick
As Jove's dire thunderbolts. For but a hair   ,
Suspends the throne of Argolis. Go, slave.

   Waldruff. I do thy bidding. I 'm gray in thy services.

                     [*Ex Waldruff.*

   King. A droughty lover, husband, this old Zeus,
To leave thee in thy brazen tomb. No kindness.
No wedding tour. O wicked, foolish girl!
But, love! It was ambitious. It would wed
A god. A thing of earth and sky. A coward!
Sith, Danæ, he 's a man of all fair women.
She, Themis, is his wife. Eurynome,
Fair Ceres and Dione. Dark Latona;
And fairest Juno, his one lawful wife.
He broke the marriage vows of pure Alcmena,
Antiope did flee before his love;
He stole the wifely Leda as a swan;
Ægina was bespoiled by such as he;
He ruined Io with his blasphemous love:
He violated fair Callisto, pure;
Europa, gathering flowers along the seashore,
Was ravished by this sensual old villain!
And thou didst wed a god, a very god!

   Danæ. Yet take me back. And else, O spare my boy!

   King. Soon, soon, oh royal lady! Ho, old Waldruff,
And dauntless three, thou bear'st the chest, the coffer.

   Waldruff. And 't is heavy as three giants might lug.

   Danæ. O father! Wise reputed king of Argos—

   King. Now! Off the cover! Ah, 't is well. A tomb
Of wood! Now force the fortieth wife of Zeus

Beneath the lid!
  Perseus.   O mamma, mamma, I—
  Dame. Oh good my child, my Perse darling, I—
  King. Dost crowd her in? Ha, ha, 't is so. Now, child,   *
Thou youngling rival to a king, hie in.
  Perseus. Yes, for mamma calls me.
  Waldruff. She 's in. He 's in. The cover 's down.
  King. Thy work 's well done. The sea shall drown their cries.
Now lock the cover. Drive a hundred nails.
Oh! wicked men and lusty workers, there,
'T is done! Their smothered cries are fainter, fainter.
Now Waldruff, Harduff, Scarduff, and old Carduff,
Bear forth the coffer. There! And quick, quick, quick!
And hurl the coffer, mother, child and all,
Into the sea. Ha! There they float! To sink?
To rise? To die? To live? Let time decide.
  Waldruff. They sink, they sink!
  Harduff. O hear them scream.
  Scarduff. A salty grave.
  Carduff. Oh pity, pity!   [*Ex. all four.*
  King. Get hence. They sink, they sink! O hear them scream!
A salty grave. Oh pity, pity. Bah!
And let them sink. A kingdom 's thus redeemed.
And foolish old Acrisius holds the throne!
Ha! Foolish! Imbecile! In dotage! Weak!
                      [*Thunder and lightning.*
A storm at sea. The thunderbolts of Zeus
Have struck the earth. Great Jove! The lightning. I—
                    [*Receives a shock and falls.*
          Curtain falls.

ACT V.

SCENE I.

The island of Seriphus. Dictys, a fisherman.

  Dictys. Was never such a fisherman as I?
For by the gills of all the fish e'er caught,
I 've had my day with rod and line and spear;
And 't is no fisher's story when I say,
I 've beat the world at fishing. An' I 've caught 'em
In rudest manner. With the blanket so,
And with the spears. With many a wiery trick,
I lying on the slimy rocks. With sheepskin,
And well-made leister, spurious and illegal,
I 've caught 'em. All is fair in love and war,
And so in fishing. Fish soliloquies
Are rare, but here 's soliloquy that 's fishy.
I 've captured salmon, an' have swapped 'em too,
For hunter's meat, as I 'd no art with guns.
An' here 's the list: "T is salmon, cod and soles,
With turbot, mack'rel, shad and green old lobsters,
An' pearly oysters bright as ladies' eyes.
I 've caught 'em too with nets. I 've fished for haddock,
And cod and ling and hake, the aldermanic
Turbot, and valued sole. Upon my soul

Have I. And eels that wriggle as they fry.
Crustacean crabs have known old Dictys's art.
I've dredged, I've dived, I've snared, I've baited 'em:
I've fished through spawning seasons, an eye on
The law. Gray cadgers oft have hawked my catch.
Sardines I've scooped. In lakes and ponds and rivers
I've dropped my hook. I've fished from boat and shore,
From log and plank. For Mediterranean tunnies,
Anchovies, and rare eels at mouth of Po.
And shad, egad! With silver, sparkling scales;
But ne'er a whale caught I, though once a sturgeon
Near gobbled me. Some fishes' snouts are short,
Prolonged, abbreviated. Fishes' teeth
Are rootless, fastened to the bones instead.
Some fish are toothless like to brother Dictys.
But, out upon me for a parasitic
Fish-louse, what do I see? Is 't whale or dolphin?
Or Jonah's stranded whale? or kraken fabled?
But ne'er did sea have such a fish. 'T is shaped
Like box or cedarn coffer, and hast easy,
Lumbering unfish-like gait. My bait 's for infants
Not monsters. 'T would require a cow for bait.
But he now, Dictys, throw thy welded nets,
And haul as thou wast Hercules with twelve
Hard labors to perform. Now Sea! Seriphus!
Behold the wonder of the world. A box-fish!
Who 'll classify? By all the scales of fishdom,
It needs an ox to draw thee forth. But, Dictys,
Again! Dost pull? Let tackle snap and cordage
Heave, heave away. 'T is done! Now stands a hero
That Felddaff shalt emblazon in old brass.
By all the anglers dead, what heard I? Box-fish,
With second Jonah in its wooden entrails,
Has sailed from ports unknown, and now is stranded
On island of Seriphus. Were I coward
Then had I fled; for sure as fish do swim,
I hear a human voice within this fish,
And 't is a mother's voice, for it does say:
There, Perse, wipe thy tears, thy mother 's with thee;
And what is stronger than a mother, Perse?
By all my tackle and old fish-lies told,
I 'll pierce the belly of this wooden fish,
And though his bowels hold a wooden horse
With armèd men, I 'll have them forth instanter.
A hundred nails! But here 's my rusty claw-bar.
As long as bait would wait for bite, wait thou.
O wondrous occupants of such a fish
As this, and Dictys' arm shall let thee out.
A pry, a twist, a yank, a lurch and fish's
Back is off. But Jove and greater Hercules,
What do I see? A mother and her child!
Come forth. 'T is Dictys, island of Seriphus.   [They appear.
But thou art lovely as a mermaid queen,
Thou art a queen, and gasping boy has lines
Of kingly greatness. Wicked stars, art dying?

Dana.   Not dying nor prepared to die, but smothered.
I gasp for breath.   I pant for want of air,
And little Perse 's wellnigh stifled.   Sir—
   Dictys.   But sit thee down upon this rude old sone,
The boy upon thy knee, and once thou 'st tasted
This aged wine, I 'll list thy hapless story.
Some fishers hold the adage that old rum
Doth make the fish to bite, but I prefer
New wine.   And new, 'cause ne'er 'd grow old with me.
The wine has brought new lustre to thy cheek,
And were I kingly as thy kingly son,
I 'd make essay to have such queen my wife.
   Dana.   Wife? Wife? O do not mention.   Wife, wife, wife!
May all good angels now abhor me for it,
That I 'm a wife, that e'er I dreamed of lover.
   Dictys.   I 'm only Dictys.   Though my brother 's king,
I dare delight in fishing.   But for this
The island of Seriphus had not known thee;
For had not I so fished thee out, to sea
Thou sure hadst gone, to perish in thy tomb,
And been another devil-fish to sailors,
The story ringing down the centuries
Like Flying Dutchman, or a similar.
But, tell thy story.   Fishers fish in vain
For latest bite when they do talk.
   Dana.   My story?
And then thou art my friend?
   Dictys.   Thy watery friend,
And with the fame of catching such a fish,
That other fishers 'll die in fish-like envy.
   Dana.   The salt sea breeze dost so renew my life,
That long I 'd sit here on the thundering shore
And hear the cannonade of mighty waters.
But tell me first if this be earth or heaven.
   Dictys.   'T is not the earth, good hap, but just a part.
It is the little island of Seriphus,
And Polydectes, my one brother 's king.
But 't is a haven in a roaring sea.
   Dana.   Then still I 'm in a kingdom?
   Dictys.   Yes, dear lady.
   Dana.   Then, sir, how far is it beyond all kingdoms?
   Dictys.   Only the fish may know.   For since a babe,
I 've heard of kings and kingdoms.   Why dost ask?
   Dana.   Because I am the daughter of the king
Of Argolis.   And I 'm so tired of thrones,
I 'd enter 'gan this cedarn coffin, and
Say : Waves, flow on forever with thy human
Freight, ay! forever, if thou dost not come
To a republic.
   Dictys.   A republic? I—
   Dana.   Hast never heard of such?   But take me hence.
I 'm fresh with sharp remembrance of a brazen
Tomb.   And, e'en now, I feel as newly risen
From some old coffin.   Yet I thank thee, Dictys,
For my late liberation from the sea.

Dictys. The honor 's more than medal or reward.

Danæ. But ere thou tak'st me hence, write out these words,
And tack them on the coffer: This is would-be
Coffin of King Acrisius's only daughter,
Where she was forced by him, and put to sea
At mercy of the waves and storms, to perish,
But rescued by the noble Dictys, who
Dost stand between a daughter and a king.
The cedarn tomb is empty, but should king
Acrisius ever hap to find it, let
Him, king! dare enter as his daughter Danæ,
And held by hundred nails, set out to sea
On voyage last to find the peace he lacketh,
Which only 's found within this sepulchre.
Now, hast thou writ it, Dictys?

  Dictys.   Ay, and plain.

  Danæ. Now, Dictys, tack it on the cedarn coffer,
And push it out to sea.

  Dictys.   'T is done, fair lady,
And it dost float as though a thing of life,
Though life to it is not. And may the king,
Thy father, find it on his kingdom's shore,
And so astounded at its emptiness,
That, wild with rage and passion, he will enter,
And die at sea, a martyr to ambition.

  Danæ. Well said, and nobly, and auspicious time
Do make thee king of island of Seriphus.

  Dictys. If this should hap, 't would be a boon to Dictys.
But come, O lady of all loveliness!
And thee and thy dear child shalt find a royal
Hospitality at thy fisherman friend's house.   [*Ex. Dictys.*

  Danæ. We follow thee, friend Dictys, our true friend,
The which I had not found though in a kingdom.
                                    [*Ex. Danæ and Perseus.*

SCENE II.

Polydectes at Dictys's house, twelve years having elapsed.

Polydectes. Do honest men dare live within our realm?

Dictys. Unless the kingdom 's changed inside the year.

Polydectes. Did wonders ever happen on our island?

Dictys. I 've known me many wonders in my day.

Polydectes. Canst thou recite to me some of these wonders?

Dictys. Gonzado's quoit-work, sure, is full of wonder.

Polydectes. And canst thou cite another, brother Dictys?

Dictys. I think my brother as a king 's a wonder.

Polydectes. But I 've a wonder more to me than thine.

Dictys. A king should lead his subjects in a story.

Polydectes. I spoke of honest men. I spoke of wonders.
But prithee listen to a wonder-story.
Thou hast a memory, Dictys, like a fish,
And be the story of aquatic box fish,
Thou 'lt sure remember. Twelve straight years as time
Dost trace it, came a man to fish. His nets
Drew in a fish of box-like shape. Dost stare?

  Dictys. I stare, as never fish had shape of box.

Polydectes. Within this fish's belly was a woman.
Dictys. Of all fish stories this dost beat old Jonah.
Polydectes. And with this woman was a lad of four.
Dictys. Then brother Polydectes wrote the Bible,
For this no less a wonder than thy fish.
Polydectes. This fisherman was only such by nature:
By training he developed to a villain,
Sith he did take the mermaid and her son
To quiet cottage bordering on the sea;
And twelve long years he kept them in concealment,
Until this lad 's a youth of sixteen years,
With fame beyond the island of Seriphus.
Dictys. Thy wonder-story 's kingly, but 't is fishy.
Polydectes. I hear this boy has prowess, skill, renown.
Dictys. The gossips peddled that ere I was forty.
Polydectes. But gossips are not known to reigning kings;
They find association with the herd.
And so, 't was only yestereve that I
Did hear this well-kept secret, and in hearing
It, I became so woman curious that
I ask thee: Is my wonder-story true?
Dictys. Excuse me king! I left the pot a-boiling.
And all my bellied fishes will boil out. [*Ex. Dictys.*
Polydectes. That varlet ne'er 'll return. But such a king
As I, will put his nose about, and smell
This fine old secret out. I hear that Dictys
Is mixèd in the matter. If 't is so,
I 'll put him to the tower where death-fish bite.
                              [*Ex. Polydectes.*
Re-enter Dictys.
Dictys. It seems but yesterday, this mermaid story:
And yet she, Danæ's older, and the lad
Is verging seventeen. Abroad, he 's famous,
And he 's so great 't is creeping to our kingdom.
And last, to open ears of Polydectes.
With wingèd discus Perseus is master.
But, Polydectes, he has nosed me out.
Evasion 's but poor make-shift, and a lie
Will soon come back. I 'll hurry forth and study
Up kingly villainies, evasions, tricks,
And all concatenations of a kingdom;
For I may yet be king of old Seriphus.   [*Ex. Dictys.*

SCENE III.

Polydectes in his palace.

Polydectes. With oft-reputed wisdom have I reigned
Over Seriphus; and till now, no man,
Courtier or noble, has e'er dared deceive me.
And yet the hour is come. My brother Dictys
Has kept in close concealment for long years,
O such a beauty of a woman that
The very gods had wooed her. Dozen years
Agone, this lubberly fisher brother, Dictys,
Did fish a coffer from the sea, and lo!
It held the first of womankind, in point

Of human loveliness. And such a lad
Of strength and prowess, that my ears do ring
With his, till now, concealed adventures. Sooth!
I 'll hence to woo and win this daughter of
A king. And Polydectes's wish is law.
Keep on thy wonted course, O Throne! for King
Polydectes goeth forth to seek a bride,
To be the beauty-queen of this, his kingdom.   [Ex. Polydectes.
                                SCENE IV.

Danæ at Dictys's house.
Danæ. And yet I live. But not in kingdom's anguish.
Perse 's now grown a youth, with reputation
Of heroes. But, should Polydectes find us,
A second king will perish for ambition:
Since did he dare approach me, Perseus
Would slay him on his throne!
      Enter Dictys.
Dictys.   Ah, Danæ, queen,
I do but call to tell thee of a journey
I soon must take. So, guarded be in actions,
As Polydectes seeing thee, he 'd sue
For thy pure hand in marriage. And proud Dictys
Would soon find kingly daggers at his heart.
Danæ. I 'll stand upon the citadel of judgment,
And with love's astronomic eye so watch
The stars and other heavenly bodies that
The quick return of Dictys shalt find yet
His Danæ free, unhampered, and as grateful.
Dictys. Then faretheewell till suns do light my coming.
                                             [Ex. Dictys.

Danæ. A noble man. And yet I fear his absence
Will breed me trouble. But is trouble part
Of every maiden's life, if hot ambition
Environ her. But Perse comes, my hero!
      Enter Perseus.
Perseus. My mother, once again I 'm laureled. Next
I 'll slay the Gorgon by the ocean stream,
Medusa, Pluto, or the hundred handed.
Danæ. I know thou hast the prowess of the king
Of sports. But, list, no man but finds his match.
Come, sit beside me. Once I dared to hope
To be the queen of Argo is. But what
Did hap? I found myself within a tomb
Of brass, whence I was torn by cruel parent,
And boldly thrust within a cedar coffer,
You, Perseus and I, and hurled among
The waves, to perish, but for worthy Dictys.
Perseus. But you 're a woman, mother, I 'm a man.
Danæ. A noble boy, my Perse, not a man;
But, be a man in all thy haps and hazards.
Perseus. No mother 'll need to blush for deed of Perse.
But mother Danæ, I do kiss thee farewell,
Since now I go to win another laurel.   [Ex. Perseus.
Danæ. And may it be in worthiest ambition.
O could I feel the same old childhood safety

That I did feel when as a girl I played
About the throne of Argolis, and Delia
Did watch me with a holy mother's eye.
Who comes? My premonitions were not vain.
Are all kings' daughters fated thus as I?
  Enter Polydectes.
  Polydectes. With hat in hand and pliant knee, O lady,
Fairer than midnight stars, I come to thee
Unushered and alone, with king's attendance.
And gold accoutred retinue uncalled,
Sith beauty draws me, king of old Seriphus.
Wilt hear my plea without regalia? Speak!
  Danæ. I rise as always in the presence of
A king. But, Polydectes, I am married.
  Polydectes. Such beauty, queen! should have a hundred lords.
I am a king; but fear me not. I love thee!
  Danæ. O gracious heaven! am I cursed with beauty?
Yet once I thanked my glass that told me I
Was beautiful. But now I must bewail it.
  Polydectes. But hear me, Dictys has a meagre home,
While I have palace, hall and kingdom! Gold,
And diamonds, precious stones, with hundred servants
To do my bidding. Come, and thou shalt queen
It over all my kingdom. Answer, queen!
  Danæ. But, Polydectes, I'm the wife of Zeus.
  Polydectes. Instead of these tame scenes and pastoral pictures,
Thou shalt behold the brasses of old Felldaff;
The sculpture-work of Greece's greatest masters;
The coronation of old kings by master
Painters, and battle pictures with great kings
As heroes in the vanguard of the fight.
I durst approach thee. Wilt thou be my wife?
  Enter Perseus suddenly.
  Perseus. No! Polydectes, king and miscreant!
  Danæ. May heaven now stand between this king and man!
  Perseus. Or else a coward king shall die!
  Danæ.   O Perse!
  Polydectes. Ho, ho! And little roosters 'gin to crow.
Young man, at slightest beck, a thousand guards
Would swarm about thee!
  Perseus.   Quicker than my dagger?
See, coward king! it sparkles for thy blood!
'T will drink it! There is brother Dictys's door;
Hence, paltry knave and spurious king, or death
Shalt be thy penalty!
  Polydectes.   Thou'lt rue this hour.
  Danæ. Oh, Perse, hold! A king's all powerful.
  Perseus. Go, king! My finger points the coward's way.
  Polydectes. I go, but fatal be the hour when I
Return; for sure as Polydectes reigneth,
I'll banish thee from island of Seriphus;
And wed thy lovely mother ere the moon
Is in her second quarter. Faretheewell!   [*Ex. Polydectes.*
  Danæ. O Perse, Perse! O what hast thou done?
  Perseus. Defied a king because I am a man!

And you, my mother!

Danæ.   I admire a hero:
But kings are walled by such a greatness that
Only a king can reach them.   Perse, hence.
Quick flee the kingdom, as thy life is more
Than fame or costly reputation.   Go!

Perseus.   No king shall hurl me from his kingdom.   I,
Tomorrow, go to kingly banquet.

Danæ.   Whose?

Perseus.   King Polydectes's.   Less than kings are heard.
This villain monarch on the coming morrow,
Will have a splendid race, gold chariots;
For he 's the suitor to Asterope,
Daughter of old Œnomaus, the king
Of Pisa, whose fair hand is to reward
The victor.   I 'm to be 'mong the contestants.

Danæ.   But, Polydectes?   He will slay thee, Perse.

Perseus.   Then do I die an honored death, a kingly.

Danæ.   Who says, 'twere better living coward than
Dead hero?

Perseus.   Nothing but a coward!   Farewell.   [*Ex. Perseus.*

Danæ   I 'm sick and trembling at the thought.   But I,
Danæ, the daughter of a king, and heiress
Unto a throne, do vow to be among
The crowd to note what hap befall my hero.   [*Ex. Danæ*,

SCENE V.

The chariot race.   Crowds in attendance.

Polydectes.   All trumps be blown.   All young men hearken.   I,
Polydectes, am a suitor for the hand
Of Hippodamia.   The contest 's open
To all young comers, athletes, clowns or kings.
Mandamus of my courts was read today,
And heard ; and those that promised horses, brought them.
Each person has complied save Perseus.
What will this hero fetch as his donation?
As his accretion to the manly sports?

Danæ, half concealed in a nook.

Danæ.   I see a vast assemblage.   Maids and queens,
Courtiers and lords, men, women and their children.
But not a man among them hast the feature,
The valor of my Perse.   He 's a king
Without the crown.   But O I fear me death
Dost mark him.   No fair play, for Polydectes
Hast anger in his looks, his eye a meaning
Wicked and fell.   But open is the day,
With glowing splendor of old Sol to stay
The wicked hand of murder.   For Latona,
Blackest night, is foul mother of most deeds
That soil and stain with blood resplendent earth.
The king is speaking.   "T is a malediction.

Polydectes.   It is not oft a king in person ushers
In games and sports and recreations.   But
Fame 's such to me, and agonistic labors,
And such my fresh delight in honest hazards
Of men of nerve and fibre, strength and prowess,

I hurl my kingly mantle from the form
It graces, and as man among my men,
My populace, my people, I do enter
In holiday-like splendors, graciously.
Gladiatorial sports, and games and contests,
Athletic haps and manhood's high endeavors,
Coupled with offered prizes, do attract
A mighty concourse, made of every hue,
And shade and color, style and worth and valor,
Especially if prize be lady's beauty.
As beautful Asterope is prize,
I, Polydectes, now do enter lists
Of tournament, to win this queen of beauty,
If crownèd kings be mightier than their subjects.
    Enter Dictys.
    Dictys. Ah! Danæ fair, what hap that takes thee here?
    Danæ. For Perse. In the distance men are drawn
As if for battle. But it will be bloodless,
For 't is but an agonistic tournament,
The prize, fair Hippodamia. The chariot
Race. See! They start! O splendid age of song
And valor, love and native greatness! I
A man and I had joined their manly sports.
    Dictys. But see! Thy Perse nears the goal. He 'll win.
Yet, heavens! the mad king rideth o'er him! See!
    Danæ. 'T was but a kingly plot to kill my Perse.
But yet he rises. He 's unharmed. But stop!
He 's seized. The guards have pinioned him — O quick!
    Dictys. The guards have ta'en him, and the crowd doth follow.
    Danæ Quick, quick! Let 's to the trouble ere the king
Do slay him, as he lately threatened, Dictys!
    Dictys. Then follow, for a king in wrath is coward.
                    [Ex. Danæ and Dictys.
                SCENE VI.
    Perseus in prison.
    Perseus. O prison bars I stand alone with thee,
And as I look upon the gay plateau,
Now trodden by the kingly sports, I see
The plot. 'T was thus to murder me in jest,
It failing, heavy hands were laid upon me,
And under curt pretense, they shackled me.
But, rusty bars and odors foul, my mother 'll
Rescue me, and before the dawning hours.
For woman's mind once made 't will never rest
Till satisfied. And Dictys is her friend.   *[A scraping noise.*
That sound? The rusty key that locked me here?
Ah, yes. For swings the door, and grimly jailor—
Ho, Dictys! It is you? The king will flail thee.
    Dictys. I have no hap for king or subject. Come!
Thy mother's wit has given thee thy freedom.
She bribed the jailor with a kiss. But come.
    Perseus. I follow thee, though much I fear thy safety.
    Dictys. My brother is the king, but I 've the wit.
    Perseus. Then led by wit we 'll bid the king farewell.
                    [Ex. Perseus and Dictys.

Enter Polydectes.
Polydectes. The fledgling's caged! Tomo'row will I say:
Young hero, thou shalt have thy liberty
If thou wilt promise me thy mother's hand.
Ha, ha, I'll hence this moment and make truce
With Danaë. She's a jewel from a crown!
A few short steps and she'll delight my eyes!
A few short hours and she'll become my wife! [*Ex. Polydectes.*

SCENE VII.

At Dictys's house. Dictys, Perseus and Danaë.

Danaë. O noble Dictys, thou hast rescued him,
A thousand benedictions on thy head.
Dictys. 'T was woman's wit.
Danaë.   And yet thou hast my thanks.
But you, my Perseus, hence. The moments fly.
Perseus. But whence?
Danaë.   O anywhere from out this kingdom.
Perseus. To Ethiopia?
Danaë.   Ay, so 't be not here.
Dictys. And hurry, hurry! Guards will soon be on us.
Perseus. Adieu then, mother, and adieu then, Dictys,
For I will hence and be an Ethiope. [*Ex. Perseus.*
Danaë. And God give speed and life's most prosperous journey.
Dictys. And do thou follow on the wings of Thea;
For even now I fear my brother's presence. [*Heavy steps.*
Danaë. That sound! I hear a human footstep. I—
Enter Polydectes unannounced.
Polydectes. Beauty has caused this seeming trespass. But,
Thy son's incarcerated. Thus I hurry.
A word from thee and he is free as love.
Danaë. 'Tis sudden.
Polydectes.   Love is best if sudden. Speak!
A word from thee and Perseus is free.
Danaë. I'll answer on the morrow, Polydectes.
Dictys. And I bear witness to the verbal compact.
Polydectes. Then on the morrow thou art mine, and Perse
Has liberty. Rest in peace, and faretheewell. [*Ex. Polydectes.*
Dictys. Now hie thee fast, and ere the morrow's dawn,
A hundred miles shall span between ye. Go!
Danaë. And leave my gratitude? for 't is my all.
Dictys. Yes. Hurry, as the king may yet return.
Danaë. If he should find my Perse gone. Farewell. [*Ex. Danaë.*
Dictys. Now also will I flee, else will the king
Forget our kinship, and the hangman know me. [*Ex. Dictys.*

SCENE VIII.

Perseus in Ethiopia.

Perseus. And yet I live, O dastard king! and for
Thy treachery thou shalt, thug! be dethroned,
And Dictys placed upon thy jewelled seat,
With glittering crown and sceptre gilded rare;
Sith but for Dictys and my queenly mother,
This old Seriphus king had murdered me.
But this is Ethiopia. And this

The raging sea. How have I wandered on,
And on. O Sea! thou hast a loneliness
That sickens human hearts. Imperial,
Almighty, thou dost dare approach of man.
O let me leap among thy cold salt waves
And bid farewell to man's ambition. But—
By all the grandeur of old Neptune, what,
What canst I see? An overhanging rock!
And chained to it 's a lovely human woman.
She 's beauty's self. O maiden, I do love thee!
Thou art more beautiful than courtly Venus.
But, dare to blush. I 've come to rescue thee,
And make thee, lady, my most beauteous wife.
   Andromeda. O Perseus, and a king among all men,
I 'm daughter of most cruel Cepheus,
And Cassiopea. And they 've chained me here,
Perse, to perish by a horrid monster.
   Perseus. Then strike I off the chains that bind thee, lady,
And forth we 'll go to make a wedding. Come.
   Andromeda. I 'll love the man that dares to rescue me.
   Perseus. And wed him ere the sun do cross the hills?
   Andromeda. For thou hast saved me from a monstrous death.
   Perseus. Then come, and Cupid fair shalt lead us on.
                     [*Ex. Andromeda and Perseus.*

SCENE IX.

Argolis. In the king's palace.

   King. Messengers do tell me of approaching trouble;
Cold Rumor bruiteth that my child is rescued;
Gossips announce she is arrived in Argos,
With Perseus, my grandson and his wife,
And even now that they are at my gates.
O cursèd be ambition of old kings!
Had I as king been once content, how less
Than death had been my great career. But now,
O Felldaff! Now, O Argolis! And now,
O Delia! I must bid a last farewell
To home, to kingdom, and my high ambitions,
And hence to fair Larissa, there to die
Dethroned and crownless, but a mould of clay.
And yet a king's divinity 's around him.
I 'm now too old to note the hap of states;
I 'm now too far advanced to other worlds
To care for mortal life or furtherance
Of kingly projects and a king's ambitions.
How bitter is the retrospect! And time
Will not conceal it. I 've the halting step,
The aided eye, the trembling hand, the voice
That quavers, squeaks and breaks. The sunken cheek,
The flabby skin, the frosty hand of age.
But as I sit in toothless emptiness,
A wreck, a cordage, spar, a skeleton;
The wonted fires return at thoughts of other
Times, years and days. And my old blood doth leap
At reminiscence of the hour that made

Me king, the crownèd king of Argolis.
I see the great crowds now. The heralds, lords;
The courtiers, kings; the retinue, the rabble;
Court ladies, queens; the dabsters, knights, the soldiers;
The infantry, the military, horses;
Enthusiasm, loud applause; the banners,
The flags, the bugles, horns and noisy trumpets;
The courtly dresses, fine regalias; noise,
And din. The music. And the one great man
Of all, Acrisius, there encrownèd king,
The king of kings of all the kings of Argos,
The cause of all this great ado, the one   .
To rise o'er all, and sway the destinies
Of a great kingdom. Never such a king.
But having much I wan'ed more. Ambition
Possessed me. I'd be father of a son
To reign in hour of my relapse. But, heavens,
The tale is one to make a murderer weep!
Once greatest king with splendid form, physique,
Now humbled in the dust and forced to wander
Nameless and lone across the earth, to die
At last by him who's near in blood, my son,
Perseus, my noted grandson. But, adieu.
O queenly Delia! And adieu, O Argos!
For Thessaly shalt be my crownless home,
Till death do take me to that other world
Where kings and queens and high ambitions are
No part of that harmonious existence.
Now hence to Thessaly from kingly cares.   [*Ex. Acrisius.*

SCENE X.

Perseus, Danæ and Andromeda at Argos.

Danæ. At last I'm in the home that cradled me;
But mother dear is dead, an father's now
In Thessaly.
    Andromeda. O do not weep, sweet Danæ,
All life in hall or hut has ups and downs.
    Perseus. And he has fled for fear the oracle
Of Phœbus this dire hour shalt come to pass.
But mine's a life of ventures, haps and falls,
So, fartheewell, my wife and hapless mother,
For soon I go to old Larissa, there
To take a part in sombre sports, the funeral
Games held in honor of the king of far
Larissa. And 't will be my last contention.
    Danæ. And so I hope.
    Andromeda.   And I, Andromeda.
    Perseus. Since now I'm wedded to the fairest maid,
I needs must be in home attendance to
Help rear the little Perses yet to be.   [*Ex. Perseus.*
    Danæ. A noble lad, but I do fear his danger.
    Andromeda. Aye, noble. And his dangers are not seemless,
For he does cross his way to find them. But,
Let Perse have his youth. Old age will find him
Sooner than wife or mother 'll dare to hazard.

Danæ. E'en so. I'd ever have him but a boy;
And I, myself, would give my all for youth,
For happy childhood days that once I passed
In gambols round the throne of my king father.
  Andromeda. And I do join thee in thy wishes. Aye!
And had I power of restitution, youth
Should be thy everlasting benediction,
And beauty rare should reign forevermore.
  Danæ. But let us hence. A husband's on his way
Of beauty's self, and son of queenly mother
In younger days ere old ambition came;
Where once was animation and eclat,
And music, song and dance and courtly glee,
Now 's gaping horrors, woes and old disturbance.
But follow me. The hollow echoes of
This grand old home do fill me with a dread.
                  [*Ex. Danæ and Andromeda.*

SCENE XI.

Larissa. Perseus at the tourney.

  Perseus. I 've journeyed many miles as fate pursued me.
Were I to live my life again, ambition
Had little part. For such the tear and wear
And sad dispoilment of the mind and body,
That fame and name are little recompense.
But as the hero of a hundred tourneys,
I needs must enter lists as last grand act
To close the public drama of my life.
But crowds do gather. 'T is a great king's day.
But great or small, 't is last to Danæ's hero.
  Enter herald.
  Herald. Who 'll pitch the discus with Larissa's king,
The king of quoits, the quoits of stone or brass?
Does such a man dare venture on his laurels?
  Perseus. I 've hied from distant Argolis this day
To throw the discus with the king of quoits,
And fates decree me winner or a loser.
Now stand aside, this discus has been known
To kill.
  Soldier. Right well thou 'st spoken. It may kill.
  Herald. Stand back till old Gonzado does his work.
  Gonzado. There 's one, and two, and three, and four, and five.
  Soldier. The goal is hit as sure as I 'm a soldier.
  Herald. And cannot be outmatched by churl or clown.
  Perseus. Gonzado flung the discus like a god.
  Gonzado. Now let the famêd hero of the world,
Renowned and laureled Perseus, take hand.
  Herald. And prove the soldier's loud-mouthed prophecy.
  Soldier. And here 's a crown I 'm still a seer and prophet.
  Perseus. There 's one, and two, and three, and four, and five.
  Herald. Well done! But who that falls? An old man 's hurt!
  Gonzado. O fatal hap at such a time as this:
The fates come in to mar our public bliss.
  Soldier. The man is ninety if a ten-hour day,
And looks a noble king in every way.

Perseus. Stand back! 'T is old Acrisius, once the greatest
King of the kingdom of dead Argolis;
And 't is my grandfather! Fetch water, wine.
Acrisius, rest thy head upon my knee.
 King. The oracle! The oracle of Phœbus
Apollo! It has come to pass! I 'm dying!
 Perseus. Here, wine! Do taste it, king! It will restore thee.
 King. The fates are 'gin me. Naught can aid me now.
But see! A vision passes o'er me. I
Am youthful as thyself. A wedding passes.
The King of Argolis is married. He
Has wed the daughter of the noblest house
Of Athens. Delia and Acrisius reign
Till Danæ 's born to decorate the throne.
The years slip in the volumed vault of time.
The king becomes ambitious in his age.
He 'd have a son to reign at his demise;
But look! A great throne rises! 'T is Apollo's!
The king of Argos stands before his godship.
The great god speaks. Thou shalt not have a son,
But thy own daughter shalt give birth to one,
And by whose hand, O King! thou shalt be slain!
And so I dared to hatch a plot to kill
This son, this Perseus; but instead, the boy
Has killed the vagrant king! For thou art Perse;
Sith, tell me this before I die, that I
May ask thee pardon and forgiveness. Look,
Look in my eye. 'T is thee! 'T is Danæ's eye!
O Perse! wilt forgive me? And my Danæ,
And Delia; and O Throne of Argolis!
Wilt thou forgive a dying king? 'T is death!
He comes alike to kings and queens. O Perse!—
Danæ!—Adelia!—Argolis!—I—die—
For—thee!
 Perseus. The King of Argolis is dead!
Curtain falls.

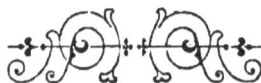

Sonnets.

I LOVE YOU.

I.

I love you in the fern, the flower, the tree,
  In meadow, vale, and pasture trod of kine,
  In fragrant woods and fields; and with the Nine
Aye love to wander by the sounding sea,
Find curious shell enfashioned fairily,
  That seems a little reverential sign
  On earth, of that far land we call divine,
Where time will never end, and love is free.
And watch the little sand-steps fade away
  Before encroaching ocean; wander slow
  Along the booming shore; while ships afar,
Like white-winged birds, fly on their trackless way,
  Or some near skiff that staggers to and fro,
  And pales away at last like faintest star.

II.

For, Poesy rare, you teach the beauty round,
  The beauty of the mountain or the field,
  "Places of nestling green," where wild flowers yield
Their lush perfume, and treetops arch around
Some little Eden, where the joys abound
  That nature owns alone, and birdnotes pealed
  Sweet yesternight, and white-fringed daisies reeled
In every wind that swept the fragrant ground.
And night came down and lit the sky with stars,
  And shed her dew on many a dusty flower,
And through the trees made little argent bars,
  That lent a beauty to the twilight hour;
Till here, dear Poesy, I would stay with thee,
'Neath heaven's constellated canopy!

III.

Sith loveliness is over all the land
  In dreams with thee. For bud and flower and bird,
  Neglected tulips, every zephyr heard
In quiet nooks, and waters on the sand
By shelvy banks, the faroff mountains grand,
  And cloud-kist, every wind-tree 's leafy word
  In mutual whisperings, each with each, till stirred
To fine emotions, motionless I stand.
The spell of poesy 's o'er me, pure and fine,
  Translucent, idolized to life by me
In revels with new beauties half divine,
  Till, like a god, I sit in revelry
Unconscious, drunk with nature and her stores
Of riches on her meads and shingly shores.

IV.

Where'er I turn, I 'm winy in delight
    With o'erabundant blandishments, now spread
    By nature, lavish, generous, till wed
To wildwood beauties, red and blue and white,
And yellow as a marigold, my sight
    Grows sated, and in visions I am led
    To rainbow lands, where Love with starry head
Beckons me on, enslaved like radiant wight.
But on I go: I love Love's 'chanting chains
    Of gold; a prisoner I care to be
With Love the jailor. Rosy, laboring wains
    Of joys are with us, crowned with Rarity!
And new delights, and maids in gossamer dress
That dainty nudity would dare confess.

V.

And this is poesy! She, dear nymph, to me
    Hast lent a thousand dainties: flower and weed,
    And shrub and tree and twig, the rowen mead
By river ways; and clothed with sanctity,
And dewed divinity and glory. Bee
    And bird and butterfly, the brook, the reed
    Of swains; the kine on hills, majestic steed,
In panorama crowd, O Poesy!
Sith, till I knew you, curvèd vert and spray,
    The miracle of loveliness in flowers,
The fine astonishment of June and May,
    The ravishment of summer days and hours,
Were sealèd books to me; and Milton blind
I wandered, half a man, and unrefined.

VI.

But, Poesy! I will crown you. Laurel, vines,
    And twisted branches, deftly studied. I
    Will twine in happy combination. Sky
And wold, and roses shall emit the signs
Of loveliness in unimagined lines
    Of beauty, classic in their purity,
    Human in all their dewy charity,
But such a crown no other crown outshines!
And so in heart adieu I wander back,
    Down, down to earth, to time, to humble home,
To dredging things, communities, alack!
    Commercial dollars, business, ledger tome;
But, gloria! in dreams I 'll dream of thee,
Translucent lady-bird of Poesy!

PAUL HAYNE.

Today my reminiscent song is sad,
For he has gone where wildflowers deck the scene,
Where Southern skies are bending sweet and glad,
And nature twines above her evergreen,
Or wreath of flowerage, for an offering rare
To you, dear Hayne! The woods are vocal now,
The meadow and the field; but quiet there
You hear no sound, nor where the florets bow
In beauty, do you wander as of yore
With poet heart; for death has come at last!
The soft sweet music of that other Shore
Fills all thy being now! The wave went past
That gulfed my crosiered Keats, and you, Paul Hayne,
Left all your loved retreats, and crossed the main!

WHILE OTHERS WANDER.

I.

While others wander, pleasures come to me
  From simplest thing, the weed beside the way,
  The corner lilac, or the leafy spray;
But others wander o'er the great wide sea,
Climb highest mountains, travel far and free
  From clime to farthest clime, by night and day,
  Seeking for pleasures everywhere, and stray
By nature's scented vale or bloomy lea.
And still does pleasure go, is seldom found
  By those who seek it most; while I alone,
With scanty purse, find pleasures all around
  Listening to nature in her solemn tone,
Listening to nature in her gayest tune,
In love with April, May and gaudy June.

II.

For 't is the mind that makes our pleasures here,
  Since tho' we gaze on some proud castle scene,
  Some old historic river calm, serene,
Or some bard's tomb where men have dropt the tear,
And tender memories cluster year by year,
  We find no beauty on the dappled green,
  In castle or the river's fulgent sheen,
If death have ta'en the one we held most dear!
To one is beauty in the daisied dell,
  To one is beauty in the tropic lands,
To one is beauty where the snowdrops fell,
  To one is beauty where, with claspèd hands,
The contrite heart sends up the lowly prayer,
Sith e'en the mind makes all the beauty there!

III.

To one is beauty by a marble grave,
  To one is beauty in a storm at sea,
  And one likes wine, and one likes revelry,
And some are sated by the moaning wave
Lapping the crinkly shores. A solemn stave
  By love's new coffin seemeth unto me
  A kind of dirge that beautifies. The lea,
Desert mirage are lovely, seas that lave
Deserted shores in sombre lands. To one
  Is beauty in a little child. To some
Is beauty in a life that 's just begun
  In honor, glory; birds, and bees that hum
To wayside flowers. And one loves Tennyson;
Another Keats; and so the tale doth run.

IV.

Some wander in a forest, there alone
  In pure communion winning rare delights
  Of mind and eye. In cloudless, starry nights
A poet is inspired. A broken stone,
No lettered epigraph, a still Unknown!
  Is filled with quiet sadness. Marriage rites,
  And rosy brides, and hoary anchorites
Are interesting, and the organ's tone.
To me, like Whitman, beauty 's everywhere;
  A larger vision came to him, and time,
And age, and æons, Lincoln trumpet blare,
  And found communion in his rugged rhyme;
But thro' our art for art's sake Whitman sleeps
Half unremembered. God his memory keeps!

V.

I love the canopy of God's great sky
  As Sol in silver-fringèd clouds, at e'en
  Gins his descent in glory, and a scene
Of grandest beauty leaves! Here let me lie
With orange cloud and silver cloud on high,
  And burning colors in a shimmer sheen,
  Now yellow, red and white, turkois, and green,
All touched to loveliness by mythic dye.
For sunset in its miracle of hues,
  Now delicate, now faint, now rarely fine,
Now Raphael-like in mixèd tints and blues,
  Is grand, sublime, and hast the touch divine
That makes the rosy beautiful! It awes,
O'erwhelmeth me, the very thought dost pause!

VI.

Still, others wander. In their discontent
  Go over seas: the Rhine, the Danube blue,
  Know strangers, gentlemen with pallid hue
On cheek, a sunken eye. In foreign Kent,
In Ireland, Wales we find them; but Content,
  Dear Satisfaction, these they never knew;
  Because, because. Ah! prophet, tell me true
Why this may be. 'Tis 'yond a poet's stent.
And yet I know me of a cottager,
  A vintner eking out a lowly lot;
He hast no want, his blood has little stir;
  The world to him is in this hallowed spot!
Cosmopolite, come back, come taste this peace,
'T is not in Rome nor undefilèd Greece!

SING THE SONGS WE LOVE.

I.

Yes, sing the songs we love, O Poet rare!
  And all the world will listen while you sing;
  And sing the beauty of the verdant spring,
Where rarest perfumes scent the dewy air,
And nature smiles in wreathlets green and fair,
  When bridal meadows laugh, and tendrils cling
  In wedded beauty, many a dainty thing
Shines out in hidden beauty debonair.
When birds have come with carol and with song,
  To make e'en glad the farms and fields around,
When brooks sing back in gentler undersong,
  And artist nature paints the clovered ground,
And all her tender forces soft conspire
To make e'en lovelier their bright attire.

II.

And heed no fashion, sing from out the heart
  Of home sweet home, or anything you will;
  For yet is beauty in the sinuous rill,
And beauty too in old historic art,
Or anything that seems to be a part
  O' man's best thought. The mournful whippoorwill
  Is sweet to some, the rumbling of the mill
To those that wander from the crowded mart.
Burns sang a various song, and sang for all,
  The high and low on every foreign shore,
The Scottish flower on mossy, cambered wall,
  The honeysuckle by some cottage door;
And so, whate'er your song, sing natural ever,
And time will hearken and forget thee never!

III.

Yea, sound the lyre, touch up the voiceless lute,
And sing, O Poet! sing the songs we love,
Like sky-lost lark, in purity as dove
Of Eden, not like Memnon statues mute
In marble whiteness, but with voweled flute,
And with a glory. Throw the gauntlet glove
Of song alow, and 'gainst the stars above,
And epitaph shall tell of thy repute!
Yet sing! Divinity 's in every chord,
For music had its birth among the stars;
It toucheth with emotion every lord;
It hast a medley in its sounded bars,
And to the home 's a beatific sprite
From heaven; so, sing your raptured songs tonight.

IV.

The crimson-tippèd flower in Burns's land;
The yellow primrose by the Yarrow stream,
Come back to me in many a twinkling dream,
And with them lovely ladies in a band
Of Gipsy beauties, fled from strident strand
O'er ocean wave; but now a faroff gleam
Of whited robes, that in my vision seem
To glimmer o'er the Sea of Fairyland!
For death has ta'en them. But their songs are ours;
So sing your ditties, sing them sweet and low,
Mellifluous, melodious, and flowers
Will shower thee, and life will love thee mo,
And when thy corse is mouldered, love of thee
Will keep thy name in hallowed sanctity.

V.

Sith but for thee, the glory of the years
Of other days, to us had been no more;
For once translated to that pearly Shore,
The land of promise, where the mourners' tears
Are wiped away, we had not heard with ears
In rapt deliciousness, of soft Ladore,
The beatific beauty of Lenore,
The songs of troubadours and their compeers.
Thy songs have prisoned fleeting loveliness
In nature; held in garlands new to me,
Evanishing enchantments, till I bless
Thee aye, historian of the land and sea,
For all the charmèd beauties of thy verse,
Sith life's inspirèd songs thou didst rehearse!

VI.

Beethovens have gin us music; half divine
 The Angeloes have wrought their marble art;
 And Guidoes, Raphaels, touched the human heart
In painted spleidors. But the poet's line
Hast foam and sparkle of the beaded wine
 In old uncorkèd bottles. In the mart,
 In rural walks and ways, we find a part
Of song that bringeth days of old lang syne.
So, sing away, so, sing away, like bird
 On native bough, a skylark in the blue
Of heaven, till every cadent string is stirred
 To melody, and crown will be to you
A country's grateful gift, and fadeless aye,
A fadeless crown for thy poetic lay!

THEY TOOK HER FROM ME.

I.

They took her from me, but I had my grief,
 A cheerless thing, perchance; it told my love,
 Howe'er, e'en plainer than the stars above,
Or my leal heart when life was hers; for chief,
To me, my grief at last. The bordered leaf
 Seemed rimmed with gold, while nestled there my dove,
 My love, my all in all to me. "Relove,
Relove in death!" I cried in unbelief.
The wedding day was set, but death came there!
 Her face was sweet although her face was cold,
For death had made her fair, and e'en more fair,
 And wreathed her brow with carcanet of gold:
But yet I cherish my unwedded bride,
Tho' best for both, I dare say, that she died!

II.

And yet I feel a loneliness. To me
 The world is empty. Broad, and grand and wide
 The whole earth seems since my dissevered bride
Dreamed off to glories o'er the silent Sea,
In hely Paradise, in purity
 Of heart and soul, and with the waveless tide,
 In barque of loveliness, with God allied
In love, and grew estranged from me, I gree.
And now I am so lonely; dewy flowers
 Waft odors to me all in vain. The rose
Potted by her, brings sadness to the hours
 Now weighted with my woe. In stately rows
Her hollyhocks are nodding 'neath my eaves,
Her bird no lilted song, he only grieves.

III.

But grief is ours. It is our human lot
  To share this sombre woe. The cypress tree,
  The willow in their mournful staves to me,
Sing only death and dissolution; not
As in the yesternight in trysting spot
  Of love and I, when she in melody
  Of heart and soul, sang out so fairily
And sweet, that all the air to song was wrought.
But now is sadness in these quiet nooks,
  And mournful dirges creep across my heart;
There is no song; I 'm sad; the flitting brooks
  In funeral dirges moan, and slow depart
Across the fell and in the twinkling grass
Are lost, and I 'm alone, alas, alas!

IV.

O give me poppies for my drink! for I
  Would drug my woe, and hasten after her
  Across the whited bulk of death; and stir
The poison wisely, sith I 'd dare to die
For love! And 'neath the unreplying sky
  Inter me by her side; and plant the myrrh,
  The flowered agave o'er her wanderer,
Myself! then dead to every love's reply.
For living death is mine. And yet the world
  Is sated with the loveliness of girls;
And yet they are not her! Grim death has hurled
  His poisoned shaft. Sweet queens and ermined earls,
And maids of honor, come to comfort me;
But nay! My tears are mingling with the sea.

VI.

My tears are falling like a silent rain
  In quiet days. And yet I did not know
  My happiness until the venomed blow
Of death re-echoed on her frosted pane
In that one night, the night so full of pain
  To me. And yet a fiddler scraped his bow
  In revelry song, and glasses all a-row
With winy lustre clinked in sweet refrain.
O what is life that I can be so sad!
  O what is death that I am comfortless!
Oh let me drain thy cup, Sir Galahad,
  Dare let me drain it in my love's distress;
Nay, nay! there is no solace. She alone
Can soothe who sleeps 'neath her necropolis stone!

THE MELODY OF BURNS.

What viol sounds so faint and far and fine?
  What harpstring echoes to my listening ear?
  Why come these songs and love's unbidden tear?
Is 't earthly muse or maid of heaven divine?
Or can it be some soft ascended Nine?
  Or rapt musician by the sands o' Dee,
  In numbers of ethereal melody,
That put such music in the poet's line?
I may not tell; and yet the numbers fall
  Like halcyon cymbals or the lutes of love,
Like harpsichord beside some castle wall,
  Like starred musician from the realms above,
Or birds or brooks in unadornèd lays,
Or Pandore gods of old Arcadia's days.

I REVEL IN THE SONGS.

I revel in the songs of other years,
  I glory in the deeds of other days,
  I love old Scotland and her knightly lays,
I love association with the peers
Of English song; poor Catherine in tears;
  I love, like Lamb, the old historic ways,
  The pomp and pageantry of holidays
Round moated castles and their sparkling meres.
And yet I love my own dear native land,
  Her institutions free to all mankind;
I know the old world seems more great and grand;
  But yet there's something here alone I find:
Since where the soul that makes the land of birth
Second to any land upon the earth?

JOHN KEATS.

They called him poet of the gods, so wed
  Was he to mystic gods of ancient days;
  So, Rara Avis, in your mythic lays
You 're poet of the poets! And art led
By them among the dear enlaureled dead,
  Among the tombs where rare Narcissus strays;
  For beauty loveth beauty. Here go Mays,
And Junes, and all the beauty sung or said.
With holy reverence we may write their name,
  Our Swan of Avon, and our Bard of Hymns,
For they are ours; we have this holy claim!
  And little halos with their vapor rims,
Are round the names of Burns and Keats to me,
Now glorified by immortality!

A THANKLESS SONG.

POET.

"Dear leafless Muse, I have no theme today,
I have no song that such as thou couldst sing;
So, spread for me your bright bespangled wing,
And murmur in my ear some Lusiad lay,
And murmur sweet as Strombus shell might say,
Or gurgling wavelet from a voiceless spring,
Where immemorial grayest mosses cling,
And earth's melodious bard still loves to stray."

MUSE.

"What mavis flying over Scottish Dees;
What skylark in the blue above the world,
Shall ask a tutor for his melodies?
E'en fountains rare in winding song have purled;
Go teach the nightingale in shady dell,
And thou, dear bard, canst write a Christabel!"

TO THE MOON.

Sir Philip Sidney sang you, lovely moon;
    Yet you were less than Stella to his eye,
    Or bright particular star in vaulted sky,
Or rosy blooming by some poet Doon,
The migratory albatross or loon
    That soars above the wave. With eyes undry,
    He sang her loveliness. The flowers may die;—
She lives like music from some old bassoon.
Aye lives in melody and melodious verse;
    For all the music of their love lives on;
The winds, the flowers, the stars do still rehearse
    Their fadeless beauty; for their love was dawn,
Was day, was starry night, Arcadian wold;
For Stella still means love; can love grow old?

READING SONNETS.

I.

I read the sonnets rare of many bards
    Last eve; of Keats, on Chapman's Homer fine;
    Of Milton's blindness and his thoughts divine:
Opening each book like pack of fairy cards,
With expectations of delight; in yards
    Of myriad flowers wandering, as the Nine
Had drowsed in sweets, like love-led Abelards.
Of Hartley's birth in sonnet's placid way,
    By poet-father, who was powerless
To see this babe would live to sing a lay
    Now celebrated for its loveliness;
And all the charms these poet-hands have wrought,
Touched into lasting loveliness of thought!

II.

So, I may revel 'mong my sonnet-books,
  And be fastidious as I please ; may choose
  The lines of grandeur, may reject, refuse,
Go any course I will, like snow-made brooks,
Or straying lambkins with their empty looks,
  Or rambling schoolgirl thro' the evening dews,
  Or sport with Amaryllis, Virgil's muse,
Since beauty's often hid in little nooks.
And so with sonnets ; they are viands rare,
  A little grotto filled with sweets ; a cave
Of silver sparkles, facets fashioned fair,
  A honeycomb of beauties, tingèd wave,
A dream of Faery. Such to me the sonnet,
A carcanet with jewels strung upon it !

EARTH IS NEVER OLD.

I.

The glorious earth to me is never old,
  'Tis always just as beautiful to me,
  With stream and runnel, the imperial sea,
The morning sun a great round disk of gold,
The mountains hoar, and in their grandeur bold,
  The great grand skies that overcanopy
  Dear evening fields, the undulating lea,
The meadow, brook, the hill, the wooded wold.
Both day and night, and winter too, and eve,
  When moon and stars are looking palely down,
When wintry winds thro' old cathedrals grieve,
  And candle lights are sparkling in the town,
At any time ; for earth is never gray,
Is never old, tho' numbering many a day.

II.

At morn I wander through the silvery field,
  I pluck the dewy flower beside the way,
  The birds around me pipe their cadent lay ;
The same old song for centuries has pealed ;
And yet no poet's lip can e'er be sealed
  To all earth's beauty ! Flower and leaf display
  Their oft-repeated loveliness ; yet they
Still win with some new beauty just revealed.
Since e'en the grass or roadway's lowly weed,
  The humblest thing that by the stile may grow,
But has a right to share a little meed
  Of praise ; since not the lowliest flower may blow
But has some hint suggestive of the tomb
Thro' which we go to Life beyond the Gloom !

III.

No bard will e'er upbraid you for your years,
  That you repeat the lily and the rose,
  That June is June, and will be to the close,
That May is May, and April smiles in tears,
That Fall is Fall with all his yellow ears.
  That March is March with clatter, storms and blows,
  That Autumn has his old-time barley rows,
And every former beauty reappears.
For repetition is your beauty, Earth!
  With rapt anticipation we may seek
The flower of May, the rose of June, their birth
  Is still assured. We climb some towering peak,
And down the Southway nitid Spring we see
Coming this way with pomp and heraldry!

IV.

And were it otherwise how strange 't would seem!
  Just paint the beauty of the rose untold,
  The pink and pansy and the marigold,
The lilies that with little lights do beam,
The world of flowers in evanescent gleam:—
  How much more beauty that their tale is told!
  Repeated; for we welcome them as old,
As some returning friend who crossed the Stream.
And are they not more lovely that we know
  Their beauty ere they come? For beauty 's more
When coupled with our love. So, starry blue,
  Still smile as was your wont; tell o'er and o'er,
O Earth! your grand old tale; for such your worth
You cannot cloy by Spring's repeated birth!

THE MUSICAL SONNETS.

I love the sonnet's grand majestic sweep,
  I love its glory and its grandeur rare,
  The poet's chiseled beauties builded there,
Unravished loveliness enthralled in sleep,
Where all things rarely beautiful may keep
  A quiet sweetness, like some Grecian fair
  In old Carrara marble, with the air
That consecrates the spot where poets weep!
The music-sonnets lack sonorous swell
  Of organ numbers from some Milton hand,
  The solemn dignity of Christ's farewell,
  The glory of the mountains of the land,
The booming of the everlasting sea,
And grand old Wordsworth's bowed sublimity!

WHAT IS BEAUTY?

'T is spring, when flowers have deckt the laughing wold,
'T is summer, when 't is dreaming into fall,
'T is autumn, when the corn is grand and tall,
And yellow pumpkins look like balls of gold,
And nature is perfection to behold,
And God's great sun is shining over all,
As this grand earth were his great banquet hall,
With feast that kings knew not in days of old.
So also 's beauty in the laughing child,
The bride who 's won by Cupid's golden love,
The gray old mother years have made so mild;
The stars, the moon, the great blue skies above;
And beauty 's in the mind we cannot see,
In tempests, calms, and Christ at Galilee.

TO LOVE.

To love is glory, grandeur and renown,
To have this soul enwrapt in human clay,
To have these eyes that tell the night from day,
Whether our face be olive, black or brown;
'T is God that smiles upon us in the town,
The city, hamlet, hovel by the way;
So we are kings when He becomes our stay,
Whether the rich man or the poor man frown.
So, simply being is a wondrous thing,
To love, exist, is something half divine;
No drowsy summer or empurpled spring,
Is half the wonder to the spirit fine
That sees the great eternal mind of man,
And comprehends the vastness of the plan.

WHAT IS LOVE?

'T is something nameless; something we must know
By loving; even then we do not feel
Its true reality; quietly it may steal
Across our being; not like sudden blow,
But half unconscious as a stream might go
Through quiet meadows; 't is incisive; weal
And woe are hindrance never; 't will appeal
To all, in palace, hut or bungalow.
So, maiden, you may love but cannot solve;
So, happy youth, your art is just as vain,
Like satellites with love you may revolve;
And yet this love your love can ne'er explain;
You love him, and the happy tale is told,
And he loves you; if love, 't will ne'er grow old.

SONNETS ON SPRING.

I.

The robin redbreast tells me spring is here;
    The fleeting snows have left the hillsides bare,
    So I can see that spring is everywhere;
And so proclaims the lusty chanticleer,
The full-voiced brooks that cross the crinkled mere.
    And happy children by their faces fair;
    For everything's a country, springtide air,
With Southern Zephyrus to glad the year.
So, Spring! all hail thou poet's beauteous child,
    All hail with beauty and thy fragrance new;
And though you come as thousand times before,
You find the same old welcome to our shore.

II.

Whence cometh all this odor rich and rare?
    This hindered freshness on the whispering gale?
    From nook and haunt and flowerless intervale?
With nature trickt in green and debonair?
The heifer sniffs the circumambient air;
    While gentler breezes, with a sobbing wail,
    Invite the higher tastes of man. Unveil
My maid of spring, and touch her golden hair!
The immemorial years have made you, Spring!
    We know you by the airy freshness round,
By robin redbreast with empurpled wing,
    By sturdy wildflowers peeping from the ground,
And brook and bird and tenderly clinging vine,
With intimations of a hand divine.

III.

Hark! every vestige of the snow has fled,
    And vernal breezes pipe adown the way;
    For spring has come with bird and sylvan lay,
With vocal voices; while with tints o'erhead,
The skies o'ercanopy with glow of red,
    Both field and fell; for spring is here today,
    The spring of April not of verdant May,
And with the beauty as a bride that 's wed.
But, Spring, we knew you would return; since years
    From Southways you have come with joy and song,
With nature's smile and April's sparkling tears,
    While in thy train a merry Paphian throng
Is crowned with flowers and vines and new delights,
With little emerald kings and rural knights.

IV.

With harp and timbrel and the strìngèd lyre,
  With rare old melodies to me divine,
  As some sweet singer on his native Rhine,
Or myriad birdnotes in a rebel choir,
Rebelling 'gainst old Winter's cold attire
  Of sparkling white: so cometh spring with nine
  Fair muses, Bacchus leading with red wine
Across new fields in dainty love's desire.
So, Winter, haste thee, haste thee on thy way,
  For spring is coming like a decorous bride,
With tepid gales and balms and vocal lay,
  With heavenly kinship, lucent, sanctified,
With no distinction for the high or lowly,
But given with the love that bards call holy.

V.

O harbinger of glory and delight!
  O deckèd Princess, born upon this day!
  O crowning beauty all along the way!
New drest with beauty of the starry night,
And with the beauty of a mountain height,
  Where Spring and Winter struggling in delay,
  Have waged unequal battle, till away
The vanquished Winter hurries in his plight!
All hail, all hail, we greet you with our song,
  We greet you as a newborn harbinger
Of daft delights, as all your beauties throng
  Our walks, the racy scents of juniper,
And newest flowers, and herald birds on wing,
To tell thy advent 'gan, O beauteous Spring!

VI.

Unhappy Spring! thy fields are white with snow,
  And Boreal blasts are stabbing right and left,
  And e'en the hidden wildflower in the cleft,
And pussy-willows swaying to and fro,
And Eden houseplants in some bungalow,
  Are all a-tremble, for is spring bereft
  Of all her beauty sweet and rare and deft;
Since Winter blows his blasts of long ago.
But see! The great round sun has topt the hill,
  And Southern breezes from a milder clime,
Have put a music in the snowy rill,
  And made of winter such a trental rhyme,
He goes a-scampering on his aqueous ways,
While robin-Spring 'gan pipes Alemanian lays!

VII.

With all the grace of beauty, glistering Spring,
  Thou 'gan hast come from climes of Paradise,
  And in habiliments so ruffed and nice,
With spicy odors borne on fairy wing,
That, like a tendril, love dost round thee cling,
  Tho' still in coves the lingering shreds of ice,
  In treachery bold, the tepid gales entice,
Now led by Zephyr airily curveting.
But, lo! dost come arrayed in loveliness,
  And wafted by a thousand melting gales,
With rosy boys and maids in love's distress,
  Who wing adown old Winter's intervales,
Till not a vestige of the ice remains,
And thou art queen of plagal caves and plains.

VIII.

Now prankt in beauty and in garlands rare,
  A holiday-like loveliness indeed,
  With Psyche and fair Venus in the lead,
And rosy gods in many a winding pair,
With balmy gales o'erlading all the air,
  Comes Spring! A thousand welcomes and our meed,
  And Fauns pipe canticles on alcyon reed,
That Spring has come, and bloometh everywhere!
But so it is. We knew you would return,
  As sure as March or May or regal June,
And with the cadence of the Scottish hern,
  And rare old viols touched to perfect tune;
For such has been and ever yet will be;
So, welcome Spring, with voweled songs to thee!

IX.

Has summer such a loveliness? or fall?
  Or autumn with his hoary fields of grain?
  Or winter with his whiteness on the plain?
As Spring with vinelets for a coronal?
With starting flower beside some crannied wall?
  Or venturing vine in many a winding chain?
  With such an odor that the heart would fain
Have spring forever, ever unto all;
For Spring, dear Spring, thou art like Beauty's self,
  Thy horn of Plenty 's rounded to the brim,
You dance across the heart like fairy elf;
  And while my eyes with dewy love are dim,
I sing: Thou art the queen-child of the year!
'T is poet's wish that thou wert always here!

X.

With naked hills, and meadows sere and bare;
  With desolation on the field and fell;
   The waiting ant within her meagre cell,
Comes pageant Spring, with such a balmy air,
And such a melting freshness everywhere.
  The heart is gladdened by a magic spell,
   And by the beauty as a Christabel
Had stept from heaven this loveliness to share!
But Winter knew your gladdened time was near,
  And days agone he beat a cold retreat,
And birds sang out: The nectared Spring is here,
  And in a vocal unison so sweet,
So deft, you drove your chariot-team more fast,
Till came the chorus: Spring is here at last!

L' ENVOY.

XI.

O dainty Spring!   O Sonnet just as rare!
  Forgive the bard that joined you heart and hand;
   Sith, loving both, where Northern skies expand,
He could but join you in your beauty there!
So, through the field and every floweret's lair,
  In sparkling nook or grotto quaint and grand,
   He led you, till a merry minstrel band
Played melic pipes, and sang divinest air.
So, may you, Spring, and Sonnet just as chary,
  Go on together, shining like a star!
Beauty and beauty coming here to marry,
  Beauty and beauty in a bridal car!
And onward so, till summer's odors drown you,
And onward so, till summer's roses crown you!

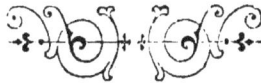

Miscellaneous Poems.

AL SIRAT.

I

Was ever a bridge as dainty as this?
As Al Sirat, the Bridge of Bliss?
No gauzy web of a spider so fine,
Spun to Heaven in a silver line,
Could be as nice as the bridge I write!
Over the chasm it swayed by night,
Over the gulf when the moon was bright,
Dainty and delicate as e'er was dreamed,
This rare old bridge to Islam seemed!
So, would you cross to Paradise,
Cross this bridge and cross in a trice,
You needs must be a perfect soul,
For only such can reach the goal.

II.

This was the way to Heaven for all
Who 'd wear the starry coronal;
So, do you wonder came they far?
Came from Thebes and Zanzibar?
From China and the Orient?
From ancient Ind and ancient Ghent?
Islam, Greek and Cornish prince;
Never a crowd was greater since!
Some in rags and some in robes;
Some with burthens like Atlas globes;
But all had come to Al Sirat;
Come as beggars, though men at that;
All for reason that here alone
Heaven's pure light in beauty shone.

III.

And yet they came, the high and low,
Over this wonderful bridge to go;
Since over hell-fire's yawning abyss
It led to heaven from a world like this;
They came in chariots silver bright,
They rode on steeds bedizened white;
But who could blame them? Wasn't it here
That far way heaven seemed more near?

IV.

But ah! I fear me, Al Sirat
Is not the Paradise whereat
Fame or greatness can win its way,
For virtue alone without display.
Can cross the bridge of Al Sirat;
And yet how proudly the noblemen sat
In gaudy carriages, their ladies as fair
As earth Madonnas, debonair!

V.

It seemed a pity to leave their gold,
Earl and count and baron old;
But over the bridge of Al Sirat
None could pass for dross like that;
And yet they came, both lady and maid,
King and Mikado in gold arrayed,
Captain and colonel and brigadier,
Emperor and Empress and English peer,
And came the widow who gave the mite,
She crossed the bridge like a ray of light!

VI.

Earls and counts came two by two,
A maiden was there with broidered shoe,
A lawyer and judge were hand in hand,
Some in carriages great and grand;
The earls and counts fell one by one
The spider-bridge was so finely spun,
And the pretty maid with the broidered shoe
Fell with the rest at the rendezvous,
Till out of the crowd that came to pass
Old Al Sirat, not one, alas!
But sank in the yawning depths below
Who came in silks and earthly show!
So, who would cross old Al Sirat,
Be clothed in virtue and all that,
Since neither gold nor earthly ties
Can carry you where this heaven lies!

VII.

Lords and ladies from old Cathay,
Counts and nobles from far away,
   From Ind and Afric came,
   And men of honor and fame,
From Italy or Ararat,
They came to cross old Al Sirat;
And so they came, they came by threes,
Came o'er rivers, came o'er seas,
From hut and hovel in regal mien,
In coarse surtout and gaberdine,
This will-o-the-wisp-like bridge to try!
And who could blame them? O not I!
   For heaven is ope to all,
   Whether in hut or hall;
If you but knock God will reply.

VIII.

So, of every kith and kin,
   Came the human cavalcade,
   Some in gaudy masquerade,
Thinking high heaven they could win
   By hiding a sinner's form

In purple and linen fine;
But, ah! the soul 's divine,
And 's tried by many a storm!
So, all the silver rare,
And all the yellow gold,
Cannot get you there,—
Heaven 's not bought or sold.

IX.

And yet they came there two by two,
Came by fours and threes and fives,
Like honey bees around their hives
They swarmed, each asking: "Who, who
Is good enough to pass?"
'T was like a film of glass,
A spider's silver thread,
A ray of light ahead,
A rainbow tint afar,
The silver of a star,
A ray from out the sun,
So dainty it was spun.

X.

If the heart be pure,
Heaven this way is sure!
So, come in gold and gilded hat,
And cross this gauzy Al Sirat:
Come in proud array,
And come, come today,
'T is the holy heart we seek,
Be it Norse or be it Greek,
For here 's the way to Al Sirat,
To man or maid from old Korat.
To men of Siam or Cathay,
To men o'er seas and far away;
So, do you wonder many came
Who owned no right to Islam's name?
Since here was pointed out,
O'er Al Sirat, the route
That led to heaven. Who would say:
"Not Al Sirat, some other way!"

XI.

Though come ye from the clime of Nod,
And from the fair Etruscan lands,
With heavenly eye and claspèd hands,
Ye cannot climb to heaven and God!
But when the Christ you win,
A million Al Sirats in a trice,
Will lead you out of sin,
Into the good God's Paradise!

XII.

But come they on to Al Sirat,
  And wherefore? 'T is divine!
The Danube or the Rhine,
  The Volga red of wine,
Have their beauty, but ah 's, not that!
And yet like a bridge of glass
  It spans o'er hell's abyss,
  I would not tell you this,
Nor give you hope, alas!
If the bridge were not a fact,
  No matter what your sect,
  No matter how you 're deckt,
No matter if gold be lacked;
  'T is not the eyne,
  The face divine,
'T is purity of heart!
A beggar from London mart,
  A maid from Persia lands,
  And old Sahara's sands,
Can cross with holy heart.

XIII.

Come with song and dance and glee,
Come old knights of Heraldry,
Come with music and poet's rhyme,
Come, come from every clime;
For, list the tale, at Al Sirat,
Dainty as flowers in a Persia mat,
  The starry heaven is free
  To sensate purity!

XIV.

And yet how dainty I may not tell;
You 've seen the rainbow o'er the fell,
The spider's web in sparkling dew,
Light from Aurora peeping through
The mists of morning, gossamer-like,
Rays of fireflies near a dyke,
  Silver threads as fine
  As a molten line
Spun by fairies in the fen,
Faint to microscopic ken;
And yet the bridge of Al Sirat
  Was finer far than these,
  Than shells on ocean lees;
And yet the world seemed stopping at
  This webby suspension bridge,
  Faint as a chrysalis midge,
And yet far large enough, I trow,

For every perfect soul to go
Straight to heaven and God!
Sweet as golden rod,
Rare as censers old,
Trickt in yellow gold,
The odor of the rose,
The perfume, I suppose,
Of sweetest human souls:
The white steed caracoles,
And yet is heaven as near
As rainbow doth appear.

XV.

The grand procession, like a cavalcade,
Wound through valley and everglade,
Over hill and mountain height;
Prince and beggar and bearded knight,
Circled round the wet morass,
On their way to the Bridge of Glass!
Over rivers and streams,
Foot and horse and teams,
Wound they up and wound they down,
Wound they round and over,
Through the grass and clover,
Red and yellow and tawny brown.

XVI.

So, on they came to Al Sirat,
Jewish priests and scribes as well,
Men of Niger and the Nile,
With tambourines and tinkling bell,
On lumbering elephants at that,
And ladies pranked in latest style,
From the Congo of the South,
Down the Indus to its mouth,
Down the Ganges far away,
E'en from China came
Notables of fame.

XVII.

He that preaches only heaven
Thro' Moorish mosque is found,
Skippeth six in every seven,—
Man's mind hath no bound!
At the bridge of glass,
Where so few could pass,
A man is but a man
From Ind or Yucatan!

XVIII.

In the rain and sunny weathers,
Some in ribbons, shawls and feathers.

Tricked in gold and broidered hat,
Hurry on to Al Sirat;
May their souls of alabaster
Cross the bridge to heavenly master,
Riding over Al Sirat!

THE BATTLE.

I.

"Charge! every soldier is a hero;
  Charge, charge, charge!"
And, veterans, every man was silent;
  But each with moonèd targe,
  There bravely met the charge;
And bucklers clashed and rang,
And targes, with a clang,
  Turned halberd, javelin, mace;
  But O the deathly face!
  And O the cruel blow!
  But war would have it so
  For honor, bravery, fame!
  And unto one a name
  That time shall garland, years
  Shall consecrate, though tears
  Were shed, and hearts were broken,
  Because that word was spoken,
    "Charge, charge, charge!"

II.

Light up the gas, touch up the fire,
  The battle's but a story;
Brush off the tear, forget the blood,
  But give them all the glory!
The dinted targe, the broken axe,
  Sweet widow, these are thine!
Brush off the tear, thy babes will man
  The battle-broken line!
They fought and died: go plant a flower,
  And let the old Flag wave;
Thou hast the glory of their arms,
  Their fame is but the grave!
For they were men, the rank and file,—
  With battle-axe and targe
They made the glory of the man
  That said: "Charge, charge!"

I HEAR THE TRUMPETS.

I.

Hark! I hear the trumpets braying,
Hark! I hear the music playing,
Trumpets braying, music playing,
  Till my weary heart is tired!
   Curse the battle with its rattle,
And the horrid guns they fired!
   Babies on my knee may prattle,
   But their daddy's dead in battle,
    Let that please them if it can!
   Better dead a country's hero,
    Than a simple soldier man!

II.

Shot and shell are flying faster,
Faster, faster with disaster,
  Till my head is whirling round!
What is battle but a rattle,
  With its dead upon the ground?
Doughty soldier, you 're a hero,
  For you shot their daddy down!
And you 're human, but a Nero,
  Tear old Glory, tear her down!
Tear her down, for she is waving,
  This old Flag of Valley Forge!
Shot have cut her stars and bars, sir,
  Quick! apply the battle scourge!

III.

Babies, babies, stop your crying,
  War and battle there must be!
Glory, glory to the dying,
  Since they die, my babes, for thee!
Let my teardrops fall and glisten,
  Let my bosom heave in vain,
What 's a wife, my darling babies,
  When 't is glorious to be slain?
What 's a mother when a father
  Dares to face a country's foe?
Battle, battle, with your rattle,
  Lay the dastard rebel low!
On to victory, daddy, daddy,
  Whip them like the dogs they are,
Plant old Glory on the ramparts,
  Honor every stripe and star!

A SONG.

You ask me for a tender song,
  Some sweet and simple rune;
How can a poet sing a song
  Unless his heart 's in tune?

I touch the chords, but in the soul
  Responsive notes are dumb:
I am, as 't were, some prison bird
  That straint has overcome.

My muse has flown to Eden skies,
  Where fairer beings throng,
And with her took my music rare,
  And all my magic song.

But yet the oldtime love has come
  That charmed me long ago;
Yet vainly, vainly o'er the strings
  My aimless fingers go.

THE WILD WAVES.

What are the wild waves saying, love?
  What are the wild waves saying?
They say thy lover's a craven false,
  That there's need for crying and praying.

I saw you come when the morning was clear,
  You stood by the casement alone,
A diamond was bright in your eye, love,
  The diamond teardrop shone.

I saw you when the moonbeam came
  And gilded the steeple with gold;
Your form was bent like the lily, love,
  A lily white in the cold!

And the wildered winds were sighing, love,
  Thro' the trees where you used to roam,
When he talked so gay of a coming time,
  When you should adorn his home.

I saw you when even had deckt the lea,
  And the moon shone over the whole;
You seemed like an angel unto me,
  With a rare and beautiful soul.

The stars shone down in a silver spray,
  And bathed your form in a mist;
I envied the starlight in the sky,
  For your beautiful brow it kist.

Your only crime was poverty, dear,
  Your only sin was love,
You were to him like a thousand birds,
  A laverock or dove!

He fled the cottage wreathed in vines,
  The tears were wet in your eye;
And all the pitying face that shone,
  Was the great round moon on high!

MY SHIP IS SAILING.

My ship is sailing; snowy white
Her bellied sails are flashing bright,
And not a star across the night
Has half the glory to my sight.

Sith in this ship my lady sleeps,
And as she sails the dewy deeps
I gather roses in white heaps,
I pile them high against the steeps.

And why? Because I love her true,
No diamond star across the blue
Seems half so bright; and so would you
Pile up the roses in the dew.

If I were you and you were I,
Sith not the sky's cerulean dye
Is half as pure; when roses lie
In dew she's fairer far or nigh.

And so this lady ship to me
Is Paradise. Breast the blue sea,
O snowy ship! In every tree
The birds pour out their minstrelsy!

MARY'S DEATH.

They laid her in the grave, and I,
Forget the tears, I know not why;
But Mary was so good; to me
She seemed the soul of purity.

I know her name was homely, yet
She had a fascination. Let
Her virtue and her loveliness
Go, would I love her any less?

Nay! something drew me; I can't know,
Nor any, why I loved her so;
But when they laid her, ah! so kind,
Within her grave she seemed refined.

Her loveliness grew lovelier,
And as I stood, I thought of her
As e'en more beautiful; to me,
At least, she had divinity!

But teardrops could not save, so I
Slow turned me back; a sob, a sigh,
A parting look, and like a knell
I bade her then a last farewell!

THE SCENT OF ROSES.

The scent of roses,—ah! to me
  'T is something sad; for o'er the sea
They buried her, and roses white
  Were on her breast, and then—a night!

Beside her grave a white rose grew
  In beauty; sparkling in the dew
It seemed suggestive of her tomb;
  I watched it in the gathering gloom.

Her pale white face came back, a rose,
  With spotless ribbon tied in bows,
Had been an emblem of her death,
  She called my name with her last breath!

I could not save her, and to me
  A sadness came; her charity,
Her love, her death, and all my woes,
  Came back with odor of the rose!

So, what was lovely, made me sad,
  I gave my love, 't was all I had;
But death had rivalled me, and thus
  Even in love death comes to us!

THE BUTTERCUP.

Who are you, little buttercup?
  How did you think to grow?
What made you turn your gold disk up?
  What made it happen so?

Who told you when you must appear?
  I 'm sure it seems to me
So very funny; yet I fear
  There 's more than I can see.

Do you know God? does God know you?
  Why wast your gold-bell green?
Who told you not to grow as blue
  As pansies I have seen?

I 'm sure you seem a perfect thing;
  But what I can 't make out
Is how you know, spring after spring,
  Just what you are about.

What made you yellow? Why not white?
  Dare tell me this and I
Will solve the glory of the night,
  The God that rules the sky!

THE DAISY.

Well, Miss Daisy, tell me this:
Why dost bee dare steal a kiss
From your lip? Within the mead
How 's he know you 're not a weed?

You 're no taller than the grass,
And less sweet than sassafras;
So, who tells the bees your blow
Has some honey? Do you know?

You 've a slender stem of green,
Only bees thy nectarine
Have found, little flower in white,
Tinged with red, O meadow wight!

With a dash of yellow. Still,
Tho' a pest, I drink my fill
Of thy loveliness, for she
Helen, living, cherished thee!

So, you 're sweeter than the rose;
Why? She loved you! Beauty goes
Hand in hand with love. To me
Thou art clothed in chastity!

DEAD LEAVES, DEATH.

Love laughs at death! Dead leaves, dead leaves,
 We find them blown about the tomb,
 By marble vaults; the charnel room,
The symbols of a heart that grieves.

The wind may whirl them, but to me,
 Dead leaves are precious, for she gave
 Her love to me beside a grave
Where they were blown, 'neath cypress tree!

So, Autumn, whirl the last dead leaf,
 I see them huddled in the cold,
 They 're rotting on the mead, the wold
Is hidden 'neath these signs of grief.

But love and I, dead leaves, and I,
 Go rambling thro' you. In your nooks
 And dells we find you, by the brooks,
In funeral heaps we see you lie.

And yet a symbol you may be
 Of death; but aigrets I will make
 Of you, dead leaflets, for her sake,
Since you and love are one to me!

THE FIR.

Time, give me trophies from the past,
 A mossy Hellas or a star;
E'en Theban splendors could not last,
 And time is dimming Trafalgar.

But, Scotch fir tree, four hundred years
 May find you hearty, hale and green;
Yet Athens fell, a Troy in tears
 Is but a memory now, I ween.

But love has lived, a cycle more
 And love will be as fresh and new;
He liveth on forevermore,
 Still spangled with perennial dew.

So, live fir tree, and live for aye
 Old Eden's love; the Garden's gone,
And Tempe, Argos since that day,
 But love still puts his garlands on.

So, fir and time, you may destroy
 The silver Peneus sparkling fair,
And Helen in belovèd Troy,
 But love will bloom forever there!

THE HAZEL.

On lyre of tortoise play no battle song,
 O son of Maia, but to me
Pipe out new ditties sweet and overlong,
 For peace has crowned on scented lea.

The god of harmony, Apollo rare,
 Descended from the curlèd clouds,
And Maia's shell, with love's enravished air,
 Tamed warring hearts of martial crowds.

But with thy pendent antler's yellow head,
 O hazel peace! I crown thee now,
Since Captain Hymen our love's battle led,
 Until we wore love's olive bough.

In misty fable thou art shrined for aye,
 But warring hearts have found thy peace;
Old war may fight his battles, yea and nay,
 Yet love and I will sail to Greece.

We 'll sail away, we 'll sail away, a crown
  Of hazel leaves to grace her, queen;
Love cares not where we go, or up or down,
  To Greece or Rome or Aberdeen.

FINIS.

www.ingramcontent.com/pod-product-compliance
Lightning Source LLC
Chambersburg PA
CBHW021410090426

42742CB00009B/1083